THE
COMPETITIVE
EDGE

MENTAL PREPARATION
FOR
DISTANCE RUNNING

Richard Elliott

Prentice-Hall, Inc. • Englewood Cliffs, N.J.

Prentice-Hall International, Inc., *London*
Prentice-Hall of Australia, Pty. Ltd., *Sydney*
Prentice-Hall Canada, Inc., *Toronto*
Prentice-Hall of India Private Ltd., *New Delhi*
Prentice-Hall of Japan, Inc., *Tokyo*
Prentice-Hall of Southeast Asia Pte. Ltd., *Singapore*
Whitehall Books, Ltd., *Wellington, New Zealand*
Editora Prentice-Hall do Brasil Ltda., *Rio de Janeiro*

Library of Congress Cataloging in Publication Data

Elliott, Richard
    The competitive edge.

    Bibliography: p.
    Includes index.
    1. Running—Psychological aspects. I. Title.
GV1061.8.P75E44   1984   796.4'26   84-16082

ISBN 0-13-154998-7

ISBN 0-13-154980-4 {PBK}

Printed in the United States of America

For my father, R. Donald Elliott

ACKNOWLEDGMENTS

I'd like to thank the many people who helped me make this book a reality:

My coaches and my runners who taught me much about this great sport.

The elite runners who graciously contributed their ideas about mental preparation in Chapter Six.

My readers—Bob Carlson, Doug Chase, John Dodge, Wallace Douglas, and Gary Wieneke—who gave much helpful advice on the manuscript.

Bruce Elliott, who helped me complete the book in this decade.

Steve Pokin, who gave hours of much-needed editorial help at every stage.

And most of all, my wife Aileen, who believed.

Prologue

"Tell me about the race." I had found him at the other end of the bleachers, watching the meet and avoiding people.

"Lousy!" He shook his head, frustrated. We sat there. Across from us, a long-jumper was on the runway checking his steps.

"Coach, how could I run like that? I *know* I'm in good shape."

"Yes, you are."

"Biggest race of the year and I blow it! . . . All that work . . ."

"It happens sometimes. To everyone."

"But why couldn't I run like I did last race? That was perfect."

"It sure was. Keep that in mind. It shows what you can do."

"Today, I just *let* people go by me. I just gave up."

"No, you didn't. It's not like that."

"What is it then? *What happens?*"

CONTENTS

Contents

CHAPTER ONE

Introduction

People who were at the '67 Drake Relays will tell you. When Ryun got the baton for the last leg of the four-mile relay, he was sixty yards behind Conrad Nightingale, one of the top milers in the nation. An impossible distance—but by the final turn, Ryun was there with him. He blew by Nightingale, hit the tape still driving, and ran 3:59 on a windy day. The next day he anchored his distance medley team to a world record.

For over three years Jim Ryun never lost a mile race. He set world records at 1500 meters, the mile, and the 880. When he ran 3:33.1 in June of 1967, he cut two and a half seconds off the metric mile record and beat the best in the world by thirty yards. Never has an American distance runner so dominated the sport.

In the spring of 1968 Ryun was shooting for a 3:50 mile when he got sick. Out six weeks with mono, he still won the Trials 1500 that summer and made the Olympic team. The Olympics that year were held in Mexico City at 7,349 feet altitude; the rarefied air would limit performances in the races over 800 meters. The experts all figured if anyone could run 3:39 in the 1500, he would win—it wasn't possible at that altitude to run any faster. Ryun ran 3:37.8 but finished second.

With that defeat, quite abruptly, he would no longer be the unbeatable and unshakable Jim Ryun. Over the next four years, a drama of frustration would play out to a bewildered cast and audience.

He began his final year of college track the next winter in an indoor meet at home in Lawrence, Kansas. Midway through a two-mile race, he dropped out. As the season went on, a pattern developed—brilliant races followed by terrible ones. Ryun won the NCAA indoor mile, beating Marty Liquori in a sensational duel. Outdoors, at the Drake Relays, he dropped out of a much-publicized race. He followed that with a 3:55 win at Compton. He ended the season placing second to Liquori in the NCAA mile final—and a week later in the AAU Championships, he jogged off the track after two laps.

What was wrong? Ryun shook his head in frustration and told reporters of the minor injuries, the staleness from too many races, and the constant pressure. He didn't run again for a year and a half.

When he returned, he was seemingly better than ever. He ran a 3:56 mile indoors, then a 3:55 in the Kansas Relays. In May came the famous "Dream Mile," the Ryun-Liquori rematch. Ryun lost to Liquori by half a step, both of them clocking 3:54.8. A month later in Europe, Ryun ran a 4:17 mile and discontinued his season.

The Olympic year 1972 went much the same—a 4:19 last place finish in Los Angeles, then a 3:57 win at the Kansas Relays, then a 4:14. By now, everyone concerned was in a state of consternation. The media coverage of Ryun had always been intense, and now the press hounded him for answers.

"No, I don't know what is wrong," Ryun would say. "I felt heavy the first lap, and then I began to tighten up. . . . Maybe it's psychological. I don't know whether it is or not. I'm going to think about it. . . . I know I'll figure it out."[1]

Others joined in, giving rise to what one writer has called a "minor industry of Ryun experts, sort of like Kennedy assassination experts, who claimed to have figured out what went wrong."[2]

Many runners understood the problem, if not the solution. A runner could be physically ready to race well, but he also had to be ready psychologically. If he wasn't, there would be repercussions in his racing machine—the delicate balance of relaxed concentration during maximum effort would be upset. Good racing would not only be hampered—it might be out of the question.

"The difference between what I did today and what I can do is such a little thing," Ryun said.[3]

This story, like many in real life, has no neat and tidy resolution. Jim Ryun ran 3:52.8 in Toronto in July of '72, the fastest mile in the world in five years. He qualified for the Olympic team and went to Munich. There, he ran incredible workouts that had everyone talking. He seemed very ready. Of course, we won't know. In a qualifying heat he was tripped up, he fell, and did not advance to the finals.

Ryun's American mile record was broken in 1981; it had lasted fourteen years. Jim Ryun was a runner ahead of his time when he was at his best. At other times, in his problems with the inner side of the sport, he struggled like any other runner. His story makes clear—in a more obvious and dramatic way than is ordinarily seen—the importance of controlling the psychological aspects of performance.

THE PSYCHOLOGICAL CHALLENGE IN
DISTANCE RACING

I am a runner and a coach of runners. My love is the distance race—the half mile on up. It is a simple sport, distance running, yet there is a lot to it.

Distance events pose similar, very challenging physical demands. Strength and endurance are required, and even in the longer races today, so is the ability to sprint. Training for milers and marathoners involves the same hard work, and race strategy requires the same methodical planning. But the side of this sport which makes it specially interesting and challenging is the psychological.

The psychological demands are formidable. The duration and the repetitiveness of distance races call for the ability to maintain concentration. Physical and mental states must be carefully heeded. Risk-taking and pain tolerance require a robust level of confidence. Breath control and muscle looseness, two more imperatives, must be maintained under duress.

Handling the distance race's inner tasks is a balancing act, a difficult one and keenly important to successful racing.

To a distance runner, the mental aspects of performance often seems elusive and inaccessible. It is far easier to control pace during a race than it is to control thoughts. It is easy to log mileage, but not so easy to chart emotions. Building sprint speed is a fairly

15

straightforward process—building confidence is not. The way to train for a hilly race course is obvious, but how does one train to relax through the near-panic felt during unremitting discomfort?

"The mental aspect," one top distance runner observed, "is the only real issue in any race."

RACES—THE BAD AND THE BEAUTIFUL

We runners sometimes wonder how it is we could run so well in our last race or feel so fine in practice all week—and then come to the next race and run poorly. There seems to be no physical cause on which we can lay the blame for the bad race; we're not sure what went wrong. I once ran a national cross-country race in New York's Van Cortland Park. After the first mile, instead of moving up confidently toward the front group where I belonged, I found myself letting the race go by. I can still see myself jogging dazedly into the finish chute in 211th place, one of the last runners. Before the race I had felt ready; it was the end of the season, so I was in good shape. And having run in national meets before, I felt everything was under control. Apparently not.

Every athlete has had these experiences, has had performances impaired by faltering concentration, shaken confidence, or the inability to relax. When these things happen, we can feel assured we're in good company. Whether it is the visible, wholesale choke—the tying up and unplugging from a race—or the small, almost imperceptible mental error of reacting late to an opponent's move, it is the same frustration—the physical capabilities we know are present have been somehow interfered with by our thoughts and emotions.

At the other end of the spectrum of performance, there is the race where everything feels right, everything comes together beautifully. Most of us have experienced these rare moments. Mind and body are in harmony. Pure speed and spontaneity are the sensations. "It's heightened awareness," says Marty Liquori, "it's a dream world, it's like riding a wave into a beach. Everything is clear and in focus, and all around me is beautiful."[4]

"The gun goes off," says Frank Shorter, "and you realize, 'Oh, man, am I ready today!' " He is describing his '76 Olympic Trials marathon. "Bill [Rodgers] and I ran about 4:57 pace through twenty miles, and it was so easy. We were just cruising."[5]

We surprise ourselves in these races—we tap powers we didn't know we had.

These races shine in our memories. I recall one race in particular. My goal during my last track season in high school was to break nine minutes in the two mile. I had run 9:09 during the indoor season. Despite my coach's telling me I could run much faster outdoors, the 9:09 had been tough, and I had my doubts.

The district meet outdoors was to be a major test. To break nine minutes, I had to go out a lot faster, and I expected that pace to feel brutal. When I hit 4:24 at the mile, right on pace, it was a full eight seconds faster than I had ever gone through before. The surprise was that it felt effortless. There was a sensation of speed—and a feeling of inevitability, as though a machine had taken over. I kept clicking off the 220's, getting splits from helpers along the track. In the third half-mile I thought to myself, "This great feeling can't last!" I felt too good. I let off—and *still* I was hitting my splits. The last lap I felt fresh, ran it in sixty seconds, and finished in 8:56. I was hardly winded. The race still has a special clarity about it, and none that I've run has felt quite so magical as that one.

These perfect moments happen seldom for us, and usually they happen by accident. Much of the challenge and excitement we get from sports comes as we search to repeat these perfect moments.

The premise of this book is that *we have the means to make these moments happen.*

The challenge a distance race poses to a runner can be likened to the challenge an iceberg presents to a navigator. Like the iceberg's tip, the physical requirements of the race are easily seen. But the psychological requirements of the race lie below the water and they are extensive. A race forces a racer to deal with the psychological as well as the physical, just as an iceberg forces a navigator to deal with its whole. A racer and a navigator may proceed, noting only the obvious and relying on luck—in which case they experience uncertainty and court disaster. But there is another way. They may proceed with a confident knowledge of the whole, assisted by proven technique—and then they will experience beauty.

Runners and coaches can work as carefully and knowledgeably in psychological training as in physical training. We don't have to rely on luck or fate. There are methods that help runners gain conscious control over their race-psych. Methods for improving relaxation and concentration, for example, are used by a number of coaches and athletes and have proven effective and reliable. I have seen the effectiveness of these methods confirmed in the runners I coach. This book will examine some of these methods, present practical applications to distance racing, and set forth a clear and useful program for a distance racer's mental preparation. The guidelines will help you be ready on race day—mind and body—to bring forth your best effort.

REINDEER MILK

Traditionally, the athletic community has paid lip service to the importance of preparing both mind and body for competition. Training of the mind invariably has been neglected. Training of the body, the easier and more obvious thing to do, has gotten most of the attention. Go to any pre-race clinic or coaching clinic, and you will hear all about maximum oxygen capacity, weightlifting, and proper running form. You will be treated to a smorgasborg of great workouts. In the popular running magazines you will find page after page of advice about mileage, nutrition, shoes and injuries.

"We are overeducated on the physical side of sports," says sports psychologist Dr. Tom Tutko. "We approach sports as a physical challenge, to be met with the proper application of muscle, know-how, and noble effort."[6]

The attention most coaches and runners do pay to the psychological aspects of racing is haphazard and almost superstitious. Coaches sit their runners down for the pep talk, where they exhort them to "psych-up," to "get tough," to "stay calm," and to "concentrate." The runners go off chanting these slogans, moving through their pre-race rituals, hoping, with no real assurance, that they will be able to be tough and stay calm and concentrate when the time comes. Of course, no actual mental training has been done that might enable them to do this reliably. And so, when the runner does poorly, he and his coach shake their heads and shrug their shoulders. The coach goes off muttering about what a "flake" his runner

18

is. The runner goes off and trains harder for the next race and repeats his incantations with more ferocity.

There are a few runners who always seem to be mentally ready for their best effort when the right time comes. It is fascinating to see the reactions they draw. Often they are seen as people of mystery. Lasse Viren is a classic example. The Finnish distance star won the Gold Medal in the 5,000 and 10,000 meter races in the '72 and '76 Olympics. The man obviously has the ability to focus all his energy at just the right time to win extremely competitive, high-pressure races. Ironically, most people can't quite accept that. Instead, they argue about whether he has been "blood-doping," and they marvel about his low resting pulse, his remote training sites, or his reindeer milk diet.

In recent years the competition in running has intensified. The margin of difference between athletes has narrowed. Consequently, runners are starting to realize the need for thorough mental preparation. Frank Shorter's comments in a *Runner's World* article illustrate this.

> "From what I understand, the guys running 2:09 and 2:08 now aren't training any harder than the rest of us. It's possible that they've developed more efficient training methods, but I'm inclined to doubt it. I don't think training has changed much from what Hagg and Andersson were doing in the 1940s and what the Hungarians added in the 1950s. Basic training theory hasn't changed much. So what it comes down to is the right mental approach."[7]

EAST GERMANS, et al.

Sports psychology, the branch of psychology which deals with this mental approach to sports, has grown tremendously over the last decade. Though still in its early stages, the field has already generated a good deal of research and literature. Sports psychologists examine a variety of concerns, including motivation, aggression, personality assessment, learning, thought and attention control, stress management, and peak performance. Their work in these areas is steadily providing greater understanding of the nonphysical realm of sports, and—of vital interest to athletes and coaches—the work is establishing effective methods of preparation for peak performance.

Much of this work has been done in controlled, psych-lab conditions, and unfortunately, much of it has stayed in the lab and hasn't reached coaches and athletes. The gap between psychologists and the sports community has been wide. Psychologists have contributed to this gap. Although their lab testing and their statistical analyses have insured their respectability as social scientists, their work often seems to be contrived and far-removed from the athletic field. Some do see the need to spend more time working with coaches and athletes, or as University of Illinois sports psychologist Dr. Rainer Martens says, to move "from smocks to jocks." Dr. Robert Nideffer, author of *The Inner Athlete*, cites another problem which contributes to this gap. This is the limitation in psychology to offer hard and fast answers to problems in human behavior, "the failure of psychological thinking itself to provide a theoretical framework . . . one that allows us consistently to understand, predict, and control the various mental factors which determine the outcome of competitive situations."[8]

Not helping the matter, coaches and athletes typically have received psychologists with great suspicion. Practical-minded and conservative, the sports people often have viewed the well-meaning psychologist as an ivory tower academic and an intruder. Some have the attitude that "shrinks" are for "crazies." Consulting a sports psychologist has seemed weird and unmanly. Psychologist Tutko relates experiences he had in the early 1960s while working with athletic teams: "One team director . . . insisted we have our meetings late at night in a remote motel so that the newspapers would not get wind of it . . . Another athletic director, fearing the title 'psychologist' would imply I was there to treat mental illness, referred to me (when he had to) as the 'team behavioral scientist.' "[9]

Despite these problems, sports psychologists and mental training techniques are being used more and more today. Several pro teams and Olympic squads have instituted full-team mental training programs. When these programs have been sustained in a thorough, systematic way, the results have been impressive. Sports psychologist Dr. Richard Suinn has worked with various U.S. Olympic teams, most notably the Nordic ski and biathlon squads. Suinn's program has included exercises in visualization and relaxed concentration. One of his trainees, Lyle Nelson, became especially proficient in these exercises. At the '76 Winter Olympics Nelson surprised all the experts with his great improvement in the target-shooting phase of the biathlon. His performance moved his team up in the competition and helped the U.S. to their highest finish ever in that event.[10]

Whereas the United States has only just started to provide mental training for national teams, several other countries are much further along. In the Soviet Union there are an estimated three hundred trained sports psychologists, at least 20 percent of whom work with the various national teams. Typically, the Soviet sports psychologist is part of a support group of scientists and coaches who test and prepare the elite athletes. Psychological testing is used to establish a profile of the ideal athlete for a particular sport or position; sometimes these profiles are used in the selection of national team members. Russian psychologists have developed, "psychic self-regulation," whereby the athlete gains strict control of his optimal competitive state. Athletes are taught self-help techniques in visualization, attention-control, relaxation, and self-hypnosis.

Like his Soviet counterpart, the East German elite athlete also has the benefit of thorough preparation and the latest advancements. Sports psychology plays an important role in his training. At the Leipzig Institute, the State's main sports center, coaches study an intensive, four-year program; nearly 10 percent of the classwork focuses on sports psychology. It's difficult to gauge how much this emphasis on psychology has contributed to the country's sports success. Surely, their progress has been clearly visible and nothing short of miraculous. (In the '76 Olympics, they won almost four times more medals than they did in the '68 Olympics, and they won more gold medals than the U.S.) In a *Runner* interview with Waldemar Cierpinski, East Germany's two-time Olympic marathon champion, we get a hint of the important role psychology plays. Cierpinski explains that his mental preparation was the real heart of his training. On the starting line for the Moscow marathon, his pulse was under forty, the same as it was before his Olympic win in Montreal—testimony to how well he had learned to relax under pressure![11]

21

Coaches and athletes are finding that relaxation, psychic regulation, and visualization are *skills* just as surely as hitting a ball, skating figure-eights, or learning race pace. Like physical skills, psychological skills can be *learned* in a step-by-step way and mastered through practice.

Mental training cannot increase the amount of an athlete's physical ability. The physical speed and strength needed to run a four-minute mile must be present in the runner in order for him to achieve that time. But mental training can help the athlete make use of what he already does have. And invariably, there is a lot more there to use, sometimes more than he ever dreamed.

Take the case of Bill Buckner, the baseball player. He was entrenched in a batting slump in midsummer, and he finally turned to a hypnotist—who taught Buckner the elements of visualization. Buckner pictured himself following each pitch carefully and swinging only at the good ones. In August he batted .405 and was named the National League's "Player of the Month."[12]

Or take the case of Jacques Mayol, thirty-five-year-old French diver. A few years ago he set out to break the world record for a breath-held dive. The existing record was 240 feet by a U.S. Navy diver, Robert Croft. Mayol incorporated in his training a combination of yoga, mind-control, and deep relaxation exercises. In time, there were interesting physiological effects. His red blood count doubled. His heart rate slowed to twenty beats a minute, effecting an oxygen-conserving state, a "diving response" similar to that found in marine mammals. So far, Mayol has pushed the record to 328 feet. To other divers, the feat is remarkable. It would be akin to jumping forty feet in the long jump.[13]

The real excitement in athletics is learning what greater achievements are possible when the body's full potential is used.

The serious runner and his coach aim to maximize race performance. They seek every advantage, attend to every detail, capitalize on every sound piece of information available, hoping to gain a competitive edge. They find that the more they know about exercise physiology, the more sensible the training becomes. They find that the more they know about injury prevention, the more injury-free that training is. The more they know about the opponents and the race course, the smarter their race plan. And likewise, they are finding that the more they learn about tapping psychological energies, the more potential is realized and the more satisfying races become.

This book then is about maximizing running potential. It will examine some of the mental and emotional interferences all distance runners encounter. It will explain some of the techniques for dealing with these interferences. It will discuss race rehearsal and the use of emotional energy. It will look at how the elite runners are preparing. It will help athletes and coaches assess running strengths and weaknesses. And it will offer guidelines to help you design your own best mental training program.

CHAPTER TWO

Complexities of the Simplest Sport

The year before I entered high school, I saw my first cross-country meet. I must have expressed some interest in running, because my grade school gym teacher took me to see the local high school team run in one of the big races at the end of the fall season, a state-qualifying meet. The high school team was terrific. There was one senior star on the team who had beaten everyone around that season. I especially wanted to see him.

I don't remember too much about the race itself, except for that star runner. For a while he was right at the front of the race, leading the field. At midrace, he was passed by two runners who had been following close behind. Then a few seconds went by . . . and soon runners were streaming past him! He struggled along for another quarter-mile, straining to keep up, but it was no use. He only lost more ground.

Finally he stumbled and collapsed. Officials quickly pulled him to the side of the course. I remember the ambulance coming onto the field and the spectators moving aside. Medics jumped out and started giving him oxygen. They placed him on a stretcher, put him in the ambulance, and drove off. I figured the star had gotten sick. Maybe he had an appendicitis attack or something. What bad luck!

Later, we learned what really happened that day. Apparently, in the days before a big race, this star runner would get nervous and worried. The nervousness would grow, so that by race day, he could be in a state of panic. It had happened before. By race time he was emotionally drained. That day he had gotten so uptight, he hyperventilated and passed out. The next week the same thing happened in the state meet.

The one thing I had always liked about running was that it was so basic. Just put on some shorts and some gym shoes and go. Then it was just a matter of who gets to the finish line first. Pure and simple. But that race made me think. Apparently, there was more to running.

When I entered high school, I promptly went out for the cross-country team. I was thrilled to be out there because the team was so good. Back then, most cross-country coaches were basketball coaches, and the sport was seen as a good conditioner for fast break and press in the winter. But our coach was a trackman and knew a good deal about running, having trained under Mihaly Igloi, the great Hungarian coach. Our running program was more advanced and more intense than most high school and even college programs. The team had some truly outstanding success. It wasn't uncommon to put ten or fifteen of our runners in front of another team's first man. That year the upperclassmen easily won the state meet. In the track season they went on to set three national distance relay records.

Besides his background as a runner, our coach was also a student of psychology. His ideas about psychology had become an emphatic part of his coaching. He was adamant about his runners meeting the psychological challenge of the race. He made sure we knew when we had "psyched out" in a race. I hadn't ever heard that expression before, but I soon learned "psyching out" was synonymous with "giving up."

Our coach was well known for his rather unorthodox methods of psychologically toughening us. To this end, he would have us run a half-mile team race minutes before our official race was to start. Or we might do a workout after the race, staying out on the course until the other teams had left. Punishment for doing poorly in a race verged on the bizarre. Once we were instructed to ostracize another runner on the team until he ran better. Another time we were asked to wear black arm bands to school because we had let down the school's running tradition.

If I hadn't up to then been quite certain there was a psychological as well as physical challenge in running, now I was all too aware of it. Our coach's methods generated pressure that we carried with us in each race, pressure that was often palpable and extreme. And although our team had some great success, we also had an unusually high percentage of "head cases" and desertions.

PSYCHOLOGICAL DEMANDS
OF THE RACE

A runner has to deal with more than just the distance, the pace, or the competition. He has to deal with himself too, his own head. Surely, I was learning that fact in a pretty excessive way back then. Nevertheless, the fact exists, and of course, it can be applied to all sports. In my own racing and coaching over the years, I've learned it time and again: The "inner game" is what makes quality performance a complicated matter—even in this simple sport of running. What I've come to see—more clearly and proportionately, I think—are the psychological aspects of performance that are unique to distance racing.

To begin with, distance races are imbued with a unique blend of *uncertainty*. You have uncertainty about the competition. Rarely do you have just one opponent. You often have many opponents and little knowledge about them, so planning for the competition is speculative at best. The non-stop nature of the race also causes uncertainty. You can't take a timeout to collect yourself, discuss a mistake with your coach, and formulate a new strategy. You have to work these things out on the run. The duration of the race adds to the uncertainty. In a sprint race where you have a few runners, each in a lane, racing mere seconds, you can anticipate a narrow range of happenings. Not so with longer races; the longer the race, the greater the chance for the unexpected. (I was at a race a few years ago where a spectator, who was either misinformed or mischievous, shouted the wrong directions to the leaders and caused half the runners in the race to run right off the course. We coaches learned a lesson that day about preparing our runners for all kinds of contingencies.) The greatest uncertainty you have, however, is about how you will *feel* once the race begins. From day to day and run to run, the body never feels quite the same. The "right feeling" seems hard to control. It is this "right feeling" that is crucial to quality running, more crucial than in most sports. You must be keenly attuned to your body in distance racing. You negotiate with it during the race, and you hope it's a cooperative partner. Your physiological efficiency and conservation of energy hinge on your attaining the "right feeling."

An impending race also can generate a unique kind of *pressure* as you consider your goals for the race, how you will do, and how your performance will be judged. Distance races are easily "graded" performances, and whenever you are graded, pressure is close. Your goal, for example, may be to hit a particular time in a race. The stopwatch doesn't lie. In a sport like basketball where you might score thirty points because you were covered by a poor defender, you may be able to tell yourself you played great. But when you are running to hit 32:00 for a 10K and you run 33:00, it's hard to fool yourself about your performance. Or how about the goal of winning the race? Given the large numbers and the tough competition in most races, this goal is a steep one—and invariably a source of pressure. Still, if you actually do have a chance to win, it's really something of a luxury. Consider all those who finish after first place. Ours is a culture which exalts the winner. We grow up with the "Number One" philosophy. Our culture sees athletic contests as tests of superiority. In this context, distance races produce one "winner" and many, many "losers." We may say winning is no concern to us, but I can't help wondering how we internalize these "defeats." How many people carry the feeling "If I lose, I'm inferior"? Certainly, distance races are humbling, and I suspect they're often tough on our egos.

Once the distance race is underway, additional psychological challenges await. Your *concentration* is taxed. There is ample time for your mind to wander. You get inattentive, you "go to sleep," and then mistakes can happen. You suddenly find the runner you wanted to stay with is now twenty yards ahead. Or you feel chilled and dizzy, and realize you haven't attended to your body. Of course, the fatigue of a race and the monotony of it only accentuate this strain on your attention. Distance racing presents a different kind of "head game" from the sports of lightning action and con-

28

stant change. In tennis you constantly act and react; your attention is forced toward the externals—usually the ball. But in running, your attention tends to focus inward. This inward focus is necessary. Plugging into certain thoughts and sensations helps you maintain an efficient rhythm and helps you monitor your body. But this inner focus also has a serious drawback. It makes it easier for you to get preoccupied and then swamped by your thoughts and feelings; certain thoughts can lead you into an even narrower inner focus—and right down a spiral of anxiety. Once that happens, running is like driving your car with your foot on the brake.

The *pain* in distance races also poses an interesting psychological challenge. We have a strong drive to avoid pain. We learn quickly to avoid things that cause it. At the same time we learn that occasionally we have to put up with discomfort to get something we want. Contrary to popular belief, there are few true masochists in the running population. Races always evoke some dread about the pain that will come. But we can't escape the fact that the more discomfort we can accept in a race, the faster we will run. Successful racing means *courting the pain*. Now comes the task. Not only must we deal with the dread of imminent pain and go out and court it in the race, but we must relax and concentrate at the same time. Quite a challenge!

The distance race poses a unique set of psychological demands. The race is charged with special uncertainties which can feed the imagination. The race evokes pressures about winning and losing. It strains attention and pain tolerance. It is a crucible which tests inner strengths.

A RUNNER'S BEST FRIEND
AND WORST ENEMY

When you look beyond the physical and mental requirements of a sport to the type of person who participates in it, the uniqueness of that sport is accentuated. To this sport of running, comes a person with certain suitable attributes. Many runners, thin-boned and light, are well suited for propelling their weight for miles over the ground. And a common temperament is often seen. Aloof, stoical, full of thought, the runner is happiest when he is off alone on a long run. But ironically, certain aspects of this same runner's temperament also can make him uniquely unsuited to handle the psychological stress of racing.

The male distance runner stands 5'10½" tall and weighs 143 pounds, the average according to one study of international and national class runners. Whereas his height doesn't differ much from the average male of the same age, his weight does, being roughly twenty pounds less than the norm. Only about 7.5 percent of his body weight is fat. This is nearly 9 percent less than other active men of the same age.[1] These figures put the runner squarely in the body type classification of the ectomorph. The term "ectomorph" comes from Dr. William Sheldon's famous study of somatypes, *Varieties of Human Physique*.[2] After taking measurements of hundreds of human physiques, Sheldon found there were three major kinds: mesomorphs, having a lot of muscle; endomorphs, having a predominance of fat; and ectomorphs, being mostly thin-boned.

The ectomorph is smaller and lighter than the larger, more rounded endomorph, and he is leaner and weaker than the more muscular mesomorph. His ectomorphic frame steers him away from swimming and football and into running. Big bones, fat, and even bulky muscles are just excess baggage when moving body weight over long distances, and so the ectomorphic runner sees many on the track and roads who are shaped just like him.

According to Sheldon, the ectomorph, the mesomorph, and the endomorph each has fairly distinct and predictable temperaments. Sheldon believed that "function follows structure." He saw a clear connection between body build and personality. The ectomorphic runner will, based on Sheldon's theory, behave in a fairly predictable way. His personality is a natural extension of his body. What is the "typical runner's personality"? How can we characterize him?

To answer this question, let's first take a look at the personality studies which have been done on groups of runners. In 1970 and 1975, sports psychologist Dr. William Morgan gave personality tests to various elite distance runners. In both studies he found that runners "are characterized by positive mental health . . . resembled the general population on most psychological traits . . . did not

differ significantly from normal limits on tests of extroversion-
introversion, neuroticism-stability, or depression . . . and scored
appreciably lower than the norm for anxiety.'' Morgan used the
terms ''looser'' and ''happier'' in comparing them to others.[3]

Wait a second! Are these the same runners *we* know? Most of
the runners we know just aren't like that. The runners we know tend
to be worry-warts, range from shy to reclusive, and get sand kicked
at them at the beach. So who are these runners Morgan is describing? The answer is these runners are the elite. And the elite are
different from you and me. The Frank Shorters and the Steve Scotts
are supremely confident and cool under pressure; they *do* have the
killer-instinct. The elite athletes in any sport get to the top *because*
they have all the strong and positive traits.

The more typical distance runners, the vast majority who never
make it to Olympic Development camps, where this testing is done,
present a different profile. ''Furtive,'' ''secretive,'' and ''brittle''
are some of the adjectives Sheldon uses to describe the typical
ectomorph, and they ring true.

I've coached many distance runners. You begin to see
similarities. Most runners are studious, their grade point average
among the highest of any group's in a school. They tend to be
conscientious and law-abiding. They're one of the few groups you
can let alone to get some work done and have some assurance it will
get done. Socially, many runners are awkward. Most Saturday
nights they are without a date. They can be irritatingly uncom-
municative. You drag things out of them. Runners are a taciturn lot,
the kind who need to be forced to have fun. They can be Spartan to
the point of self-injury. A coach must watch them like a hawk
because they can go days and weeks before complaining of a pain.
What my runners *do* complain about is not getting recognition like
the football and basketball players. And yet they thoroughly enjoy
their underdog status and their anonymity.

Dr. George Sheehan is perhaps the most popular spokesman
for the runner today. In *Running and Being* Sheehan offers insights
about ''the runner,'' based on his self-observations and long association with other runners: ''he is detached, ambivalent, reticent,
suspicious, cautious, awkward, and reflective. He finds ideas much
more interesting than people.''[4]

31

By and large, a runner's temperament serves him well in his running. The solitary logging of miles suits him. His independent nature bridles in team sports. Distance racing evokes a more inward focus as a runner locks onto a thought or feeling. Being more oriented to thoughts than to people, the runner is at home when he's inwardly focused. The runner is a stoic. He is too slight of stature for direct fighting. If he wins, he wins by attrition, by perseverance, by being the first one to finish because he is the last one to quit.

But at the same time, the runner's temperament also has aspects which can easily frustrate good racing. The runner "reacts to stress by withdrawal," observes Sheehan. "In an egalitarian, competitive society where there is no excuse for failure, he scores well below the median in need to achieve. He lacks the necessary psychological energy and enterprise and willingness to take risk . . . The truth is that the runner is not made for the things and people and institutions that surround him."[5]

In this light, many of the personality traits previously mentioned can also be seen as weaknesses—and can lead to a runner's undoing in a race. A runner's solitary nature causes him to shy away from risks. He can barely manage the anxiety that races produce in him. He tends to be too analytical, gets mired in his thoughts, and loses his spontaneity. Young distance runners, especially, drive head track coaches crazy with their inconsistency. "My runners think too much!" the coaches fume. It's also true the runner may tend to lack the need to achieve; his competitiveness can fluctuate. This causes another common outburst from coaches: "He's just not a competitor!" And although he may be a persevering sort, the runner seems to be tired all the time. Often he lacks the energy and aggression for decisive action.

Runners can be surprisingly underconfident. Even the elite. David Moorcroft jolted the running world in the summer of '82 when he blew away the 5,000 meter world record by six seconds. He is a refreshingly candid sort, and his remarks about runners ring true. "By nature, I'm not the most confident of people. Actually, I think a lot of athletes exude some false self-confidence which hides a little of their insecurity."[6]

But good racing demands confidence, risk-taking, spontaneity, competitiveness, coolness under pressure, and aggression.

In these areas many runners struggle against their nature, trying to make the most out of what is often a limited supply of these traits. It is a struggle that further complicates the art of racing.

FIGHT OR FLIGHT OR TIGHT

I am with my runners almost every day. We get to feeling comfortable around each other, get to know each other well. Comes the race day . . . and they can be different creatures, strangers. The pale face. The cold handshake. The enlarged pupils. The "cotton mouth."

You can almost *see* the gears up there in the head working overtime. One runner is starting his warm-up three hours too soon. Another is giving himself a silent pep talk. Another gets to the starting line, begins to take off his sweat pants . . . and finds he's forgotten his race shorts.

All racers have experienced the symptoms of nervousness to varying degrees before and during their races. Breathing is shallower. Muscles feel tighter. Frequent trips to the bathroom are made. Thinking is distracted. Stomach feels queasy. I knew a runner who threw up before every race as if it were part of his warm-up.

We've talked about how the race itself poses some intimidating demands, and we've also talked about some of the potential weaknesses of the runner who comes to meet these demands. We shouldn't overlook another ever-present ingredient—the swirl of outside pressures to which every athlete is subject, pressures coming from all directions—coach, friends, school, job . . . Now, race time comes. Add all these ingredients together and mix with the power of imagination *and* . . . *voila!* You have turned a fun, leisure-time pursuit into a fate worse than death.

When you perceive a situation as threatening (whether it really *is* or not), your body launches into a state of increased arousal to meet this threat. It's an automatic response, a survival mechanism we animals have. A series of alarms goes off in the body. First, the hypothalamus releases a hormone which, in turn, affects other glands. Adrenaline and other potent hormones shoot into the blood stream, alerting the rest of the body to prepare for battle. Muscles

33

tense, heart rate increases, breathing quickens, the digestive system shuts down.

This super-activated state is often called the "fight or flight" response. It can save lives, can help us smash an attacker over the head, or help us dodge a speeding truck. In sports, a certain amount of this activation is natural and healthy. You don't want to be falling asleep on the starting line. You want to feel ready to race hard and full of zest. This problem is, in most kinds of athletic performance, the line between how much arousal is helpful and how much arousal is detrimental is easily crossed. In distance racing, the runner who is really "pumped-up" beforehand often gets in the race and displays neither fight nor flight. He simply runs tight.

To gain control over your race-psych, you should have an understanding of how you change when you are aroused. Arousal is a cumulative state, a build-up of physical changes and also thoughts and emotions. What follows are two lists of some of the things that might occur as your level of arousal increases, the first showing physical changes and the second showing mental activity.

Physical Changes
   Queasiness, "butterflies," nausea.
   Loose bowels, frequent urinating.
   Fluttering or pounding heart.
   Shallow breathing, frequent yawning.
   Tightness in throat, choking sensation.
   Blurred vision, watery eyes, dizziness.
   Muscle tightness.
   Impaired coordination.
   Tight grip, white knuckles.
   Feeling of overall weakness, tiredness, or heaviness.
   Brittle feeling, lower pain threshold, susceptibility to injury.
   Slower reactions.
   Dryness in throat, "cotton mouth."
   Blood distribution away from extremities; cold hands, feet.
   Sweating.
   Restlessness, edginess, insomnia.
   Trembling, twitching.
   Superfluous movements, nail-biting, choppy motions.
   Forgetfulness, distractedness, poor concentration.
   Pupil dilation.

34

Increased heart rate, measured by electrocardiogram (EKG).
    Increased blood pressure.
Increased blood sugar.
Increase of certain hormones: adrenaline, epinephrine, cortisone.
Faster brain wave activity, measured by electroencephalogram (EEG).
Skin resistance drops, measured by galvanic skin response test (GSR).
Increased muscle tension, measured by electromyograph (EMG).

It is easy to see how many of these changes can be detrimental to the athlete. Shallow breathing, for example, may cause you shortness of breath and impair your ability to take in oxygen. Muscle tightness in your arms and legs hinders your fluidity. Prolonged tension leads to early fatigue.

Mental Activity

Just as your body activates in response to stress, so does your mind. Your thoughts skip around. You feel distracted. It's harder to concentrate. This increased mental activity is suggested by EEG tests. In the relaxed state, your brain wave pattern typically looks like this:

Figure 2-1. Relaxed State

But in an excited state, your brain waves increase in frequency and decrease in amplitude, like this:

Figure 2-2. Excited State

It is almost as if gates are opened, allowing many more thoughts to flood the mind.

Typically, you will experience both positive and negative thoughts during your performance. The more confident and assured you feel, the more positive the content of your thoughts. Inevitably, you will also have some negative thoughts, pushing and shoving and trying to get center stage. If you perceive a situation as threatening, you are bound to have some fears, doubts, or worries. An important relationship to remember is that as your overall arousal level increases, your level of anxiety often tends to increase too.

Because we are talking about the things that complicate good racing, it is instructive to look at some of the more common *negative* thoughts which distract runners. One question I regularly ask runners is what they think about before and after their race. This list of distracting thoughts is culled from their many answers:

Expectations
Will I do well in this race?
Will I do my job for the team?
Will I hit the time I should?
Will I finish in the place I should?
Will I improve?
What if I get last place?
What if all my work doesn't pay off?
Will I beat _____?
What if I let myself down?
What if I let down _____?

Preparedness
Am I prepared?
What about those poor workouts?
What about those bad races?
What about that sickness?
What about that injury? My leg doesn't feel right.
Have I had enough speedwork (or mileage) for this race?
My warm-up was bad.
My pre-race meal was not right.
The coaching I've had is bad.
I feel stale.
I feel distracted; I can't concentrate.
I'm thinking too much.
I feel dazed.
Do I have a good race plan?

I feel depressed.
My form is sloppy.
I feel tired; I feel weak; I feel tight. My legs feel heavy.
I feel too hervous. I feel panicky.
I don't feel psyched up at all.
I really don't want to race.
This race is meaningless. What's the use?
I'll look to the next race (or to the next season).
I proved myself last race (or season).

Race conditions
The course is too hilly.
It's too windy.
It's too hot.
The footing is bad.
The course is too tight.
Will I get race-splits?
My shoes don't feel right.
My running clothes aren't right.

Race behavior
I have a bad start. I have a bad kick.
I lack endurance.
I lack leg speed.
Will I hit the pace?
Will I maintain contact?
Can I go the distance?
Will I respond when I should?
I usually have bad luck.
Do I know the course?
Will I be able to deal with the pain?
Will I feel right? Will I choke?
Will I make a foolish mistake?

Other people
There are a lot of good runners in this race.
_____ will be in the race.
He sure looks strong today.
What will he do to beat me? I don't know much about him.
What will Coach say after the race?
Whay will my _____ say after the race?
_____ puts pressure on me.
_____ criticized me.

37

_____ is in the crowd today.
_____ is ignoring me.
The officials here are bad.
The reporters are bothersome.
The spectators are hostile.

Ambivalence, fears, personal problems
What if I beat my friend?
What if I make _____ look bad?
Am I right for this sport?
This sport is unmanly.
This sport is time-consuming and frivolous.
I wish I were more confident.
I feel low. I'm worthless.
I am afraid of doing badly.
I am afraid of doing well.
I am afraid of performing in front of people.
I am afraid of being afraid.
I am worried about my parents.
I am worried about my: girlfriend, boyfriend, job, money, looks,
    grades, _____.

Sound familiar? Some of these thoughts are always there percolating in the unquiet waters of the mind. Some may be clear and distinct. Others may be vague and diffused. *What* you think about in stressful situations and *how* you think are—like your bodily reactions—highly individualistic. And here too, it is easy to see how these negative thoughts can be detrimental. The thoughts might distract you from your race objectives. You might lose your spontaneity, become indecisive. You might forget strategy. Or those preoccupations can be self-fulfilling. For example, if you're afraid of a hill, your muscles have been programmed by your mind to react to this fear—hence, the tightness in your legs when you get to the hill. You ultimately are thinking more about your anxiety than you are about the task.

What is the relationship between this psychological activity and your physical response to arousal? The mind and the body are inseparably linked. Changes in the body influence your thoughts, and likewise, thoughts influence the body. They are both the cause and the effect of arousal. You may feel a little worried about your race because your legs feel tight. The worry triggers alarms in the body and your muscles feel tighter. Now you really begin to worry.

Dr. Tom Tutko offers this illustration of the reciprocal nature of the mind and body: "One of the characteristics of the 'fight or flight' syndrome is that it is cyclical . . . You can prove this to yourself with a simple experiment. Try grimacing, making the most angry expression you can. If you hold this expression for a few moments, you probably will note that you actually start to *feel* angry, even though there was nothing for you to be sore about to start with. This is an elementary form of bio-feedback. Your brain gets the message from your body that something is wrong and reacts to it."[7]

Mind and body interact, therefore, and contribute to an increased level of arousal for the race. How much of this arousal is necessary for successful racing? Obviously, the nervous system should be more active than in sleep. Heart rate and blood flow *do* need to be up to get the needed oxygen to the muscles. We've all experienced the difficulty of pushing ourselves hard when we feel no excitement for the race. We want to feel "juiced up." It helps us shoot out to a quick, effortless start. Perhaps even a little fear is good. It helps keep us "honest," prevents overconfidence. So, how much? And at what point do we cross the line?

THE LADY WHO PICKED UP THE CAR

There are many versions of the popular legend "The Lady Who Picked Up the Car." In one version the family car is parked in the driveway. The teenage son has the car jacked up. He is underneath the car, working on some minor repair, when the jack collapses, pinning the boy underneath the car. From inside the house, the boy's mother hears him scream. She rushes outside and takes in the scene with a gasp. Without thinking, she races over and lifts up one end of the car, allowing her son to get free, performing a feat of strength that has immortalized her.

In these stories, the lady is usually rather small. In at least one version, a sobering thought is tacked on: the woman suffers permanent damage to her back. But always the main theme of the story is—"See what amazing feats are possible when the adrenaline is really flowing!" And typically, after hearing this story, the listener thinks wistfully, "Gee, if I could only get at this tremendous power within me . . ."

Like most legends, this story undoubtedly originated with some actual happening and has been embellished over the years, but is still grounded in some truth. At least in moments of great duress, we know the human body *is* capable of extraordinary power.

This popular notion has captured our imagination. "If I can just turn on this hysteria, get myself up to this frenzied pitch—then I will be able to do . . . anything!" The notion pervades the sports world. It is an axiom of the coach's philosophy, a given in the athlete's preparation. Much of the traditional, pre-contest ritual is focused on getting "psyched-up." So you have pep rallies and fiery speeches. University of Michigan football coach Bo Schembechler stated it succinctly: "No team can ever get too high!"[8] The more motivated or driven or "up" you are, the better you will perform. Psychologists refer to this idea as the "drive theory." The graphic representation of this relationship is shown in Figure 2-3.

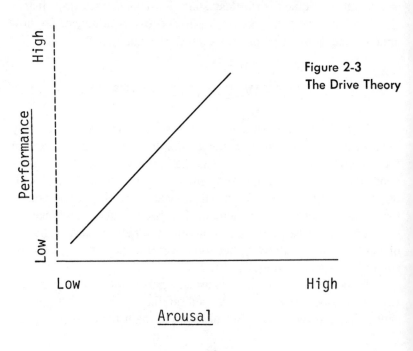

Figure 2-3
The Drive Theory

Many coaches still hold to this theory, despite the fact that for years psychologists have rejected it. Psychological studies have consistently shown a relationship between arousal and performance which is different from the one pictured in Figure 2-3. It is called the "inverted - U theory," and psychologists believe it gives a more accurate picture of this relationship. Let's take a look at a few of the studies which support this theory.

In the early part of this century, two Harvard psychologists, Dr. Robert Yerkes and Dr. John Dodson, devised tests to study the relationship between the strength of a stimulus and the rate of learning. Mice were given certain tasks and then stimulated through electric shocks to perform the tasks. The psychologists could control the strength of the shock and also the degree of difficulty of the task. Working with these contingencies, they looked for the number of trials it took the mice to learn a particular task. In every case they found that the *medium*-strength shock produced the fastest learning. They also found that for a more complex task, a lesser-strength shock effected the optimal performance.[9]

In 1934 a similar test was done with human subjects. The researcher (Patrick) put the subject in a room. The subject's task was to escape through one of four doors, only one of which was open at any time. The researcher would change the escape door, randomly, for each trial. It was found that the subject would use a fairly logical plan, going around the room checking each door in an orderly way. But then the motivation to escape was intensified— electric shocks were given through the floor. When this happened, the subject's responses tended to be much less methodical and orderly. We can imagine the poor soul abandoning his logic, flying around the room every which way tugging on doors.[10]

In a more recent and relevant study, Dr. Robert Nideffer tested swimmers and divers at the University of Rochester. He compared their level of arousal to their performance in swim meets. To check the level of arousal, he used a skin conductance test. (As your arousal level increases, you perspire. As this happens, it becomes easier for electric current to pass through your skin. A galvanic skin response (GSR) test measures this amount of conductance. This same principle is used in lie-detector tests.) Nideffer measured skin-conductance of the swimmers in the 100 yard freestyle in each meet of the 1975 season. His conclusions were unequivocal. "What we discovered was that the more aroused the swimmer, the poorer he performed . . . If a swimmer swam a 54.0 hundred yard freestyle with a high level of arousal, he would swim a 50.7 hundred with a low level."[11]

In testing divers the same way, Nideffer could examine another element. Not only could he check the relationship between arousal and overall performance (which he found to be the same as with the swimmers), but he could also check how the *degree of difficulty* of the dive figured into this picture. As we might expect, he found that "the complex, optional dives were more affected by increases in arousal than the relatively simple, required dives."[12]

These are just a few of the studies which confirm the "inverted - U theory." We can portray the theory in Figure 2-4.

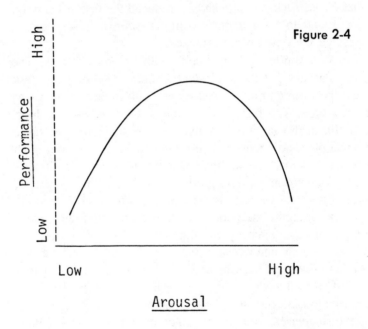

Figure 2-4

Based on the research that has been done, we can make certain conclusions about performance and arousal. Both coaches and athletes find that practical experience bears out these conclusions.

1) *Some moderate arousal is necessary for optimal performance.*

There is the story of the Czechoslovakian boxer who found that, indeed, some arousal was necessary for good performance. This boxer had always gotten overly tense and anxious in major competition. Before the Mexico Olympic Games, the Czechoslovakian team psychologist worked with the boxer regularly, teaching him progressive relaxation and relieving much of the boxer's anxiety. In his first bout at the Games, the boxer came out of his corner, relaxed, smiling, his arms hanging loosely at his sides. His more aroused opponent knocked him cold at 1:30 into the first round.[13]

2) *Relatively soon, however, as the arousal level increases, performance levels off and then begins to deteriorate rapidly. Because most sports contests invariably are going to increase arousal in the athlete, for all practical purposes, he normally will benefit by tying to lower his arousal level.*

Knowing the distance runner's temperament, this would seem to be even more important. A few years ago I was preparing my cross-country team for a state-qualifying meet. By nature, I tend to approach races in a low-key fashion, but for this meet I changed my *modus operandi*. The competition was tough, our team was marginal, and I knew they would have to run their best races to make the state final. I felt I had to really get them up, "pull out all the stops." The night before the race, I gave an emotional talk. I finished by reading the team a stirring letter from last year's team captain who was now a scholarship athlete at college. The morning of the race, the parents remarked on the change in their sons for this meet. Their sons had never been this up before . . .

The race was a total bomb-out. Our boys were pale, tight, unresponsive. Not one ran well that day!

3) *The more complex the task, the sooner performance will suffer as the level of arousal increases.*

In considering this point, one must first distinguish between simple and complex tasks. In this context, "simple" suggests tasks which require gross motor skills. Skills which entail short bursts of brute strength, like blocking and tackling in football, lifting heavy weights, and sprinting a hundred meters fall into this category.

43

More arousal can be tolerated in these skills. And when you think about people in these sports, you do picture athletes who seem to be more demonstrably aroused in competition, and perhaps for them, a higher arousal level is effective.

"Complex" tasks would be those which demand fine motor movements and fine sensory discrimination. Golf putting, archery, field goal kicking, and free-throw shooting fall into this category. In these sports, we picture athletes who attempt to stay very calm. These kinds of skills suffer first from arousal. One basketball coach kept meticulous records on his players' free-throw shooting both in practice and in games. He found that in practice free throws were made 78 percent of the time, whereas in games free throws were made 59.8 percent of the time. This suggests just how detrimental tension can be to complex skills.

Where would distance running fall on this continuum of simple to complex skills? I believe somewhere in the middle, between sprinting and archery.

4) *If the task is one that already has been well-learned and practiced, then normally a greater amount of arousal may be tolerated.*

If the athlete is just learning the task, arousal is more upsetting. If the athlete is already adept at the skill, he can handle more arousal. I learned this in high school. In my first district and state track meets I had a bad case of nerves. After both races, my stomach hurt so badly I was nearly doubled over. Surprisingly, this nervousness didn't seem to hurt my races. I was lucky, however. Both races were much like the ones I had been running—slow-paced, predictable, and ending in an extended kick. They were "my kind of races," and therefore I was less affected by my nervousness.

5) *Within these parameters, each person reacts in his own unique way to stress. Some have a low tolerance for stress, some high. Each has his own arousal level at which he will perform best.*

While some athletes handle a tense situation with amazing poise, others fold up immediately. One man's trauma might be another's challenge.

In *Improving Your Running*, Coach Billy Squires relates an interesting psychological experiment which illustrates this point.

There was a study done with a group of professional race-car drivers and a control group. Subjects in the two groups were given a task to do, first under good conditions (good lighting, no noise) and then under stressful conditions (lights blinking, horns blowing).

As expected, the performance of the control group (the non-race-car drivers) deteriorated during the latter situation. Interestingly, the race-car drivers *improved* in the second trial, with the more stressful situation. Their performance would finally deteriorate at some level of stress; however, this story does show how sharply people's coping abilities vary. [14]

Control of the state of arousal, then, is one of the key concerns in quality athletic performance. The runner must understand just what the distance race will require. He must know himself well. He must understand the various pressures he will encounter, and he must understand how his mind and body will respond to stress. This chapter examined some of these factors.

Armed with this understanding, the runner must find his own optimal level of arousal and then learn how to attain his "perfect psych" consistently. Chapter Three will examine this topic and the issue of relaxation.

CHAPTER THREE

Calming the Body

"Now, here is what we're going to do. I am going to have your meals sent up to your room. Keep that door locked. Talk to no one, particularly reporters. Now we are going through the relaxation routine we have done so many times at the University. It will loosen you up."

Evans began to relax. Moments before, he was coming apart at the seams. It was the day Lee Evans was to run the Olympic finals in the 400-meter. The Mexico City Olympic Village was in an uproar. The day before, Tommie Smith and John Carlos had been kicked off the American team for their "Black Power" salute on the victory stand. For hours Evans had been besieged by team managers, reporters, and teammates. What did he think of the action taken against Smith and Carlos? If he won a medal today in the Olympic final, what would he do on the stand?

When Evan's coach, Bud Winter of San Jose State University, arrived that day at the Olympic Village, he knew he'd have to act quickly or Evans would be a wreck for the race. The quartermiler had been up all night and ·looked terrible. Winter pulled Evans through the crowds, got him back to a quiet dorm room, and settled right away the question of whether Evans would demonstrate on the stand (Evans would). Winter then launched into the calming technique which had served his runners so well over the years, albeit in much less stressful situations than this.

"I started through the relaxation routine and he was asleep in three minutes. No longer were there wrinkles in his forehead . . ."

"[Several hours later]. When I saw Lee on the practice field, he looked loose and ready. He had clocked two and a half hours of relaxed sleep. I gave him a short pep talk, but he didn't need it."

In the stands, before the race, Winter was still concerned. Had Evans recovered enough to run up to his capabilities? He'd have to be if he wanted to win. On the curve of arousal, Evans had been over the top and down at the bottom of the other side. Would he be able to bring himself to the top of that curve, to ideal readiness?

Evans answered this in short order, winning the Olympic Gold Medal and setting a world record of 43.86. It still stands.[1]

SPEED CITY

Coach Bud Winter knew that people perform best when they're relaxed. He believed in that principle and he did something about it. He implemented a relaxation training program, first to groups of flyers at the Del Monte Naval Pre-Flight School where he was an instructor during World War II, and later to his track athletes at San Jose State. He employed relaxation techniques that had been common knowledge for years in the field of psychology. His groups of flyers on flight tests consistently outscored other groups who didn't have the training. His track athletes at San Jose set 37 world records. In the 1960s his sprinters were so dominant, track people referred to San Jose as "Speed City."

Winter's teaching of relaxation came in two realms. Away from the field of battle, his trainees learned the series of exercises comprising the routine, practiced, and got where they could fall asleep whenever they needed to and get themselves calm prior to pressure situations. The other realm was the field of battle, up in the airplane or on the track, and here Winter taught his people to apply their learning, emphasizing the importance of keeping the muscles loose at all times.

"We preached relaxation from the time the athletes started their warm-up until they unlaced their shoes at the end of the workout,"[2] says Winter. When his runners wanted to run their fastest, he

48

told them to run at nine-tenths speed. Not all-out, nine-tenths. Winter knew that when runners try to run all-out, invariably they tense muscles which should be kept loose. The result is less-than-maximal speed. The signs of the loser, Winter maintained, were the tight fist, the straining neck, and the clenched teeth. The signs of the winner were the loose hands and shoulders, the slack jaw, the "brook trout look," the "meat hanging on the bones."

Winter knew relaxation training was just as important for distance runners as for sprinters. "It is necessary to get more mileage out of the energy gallon."[3] His distance runners enjoyed notable success too, twice winning the NCAA Cross-Country Championship.

Many top distance runners cite the ability to relax as the first requisite for racing success. Tom Osler, an ultramarathon champion and a longtime student of the science of our sport, explains: "What the distance runner requires is to be able to coast at nearly top speed with unused muscle fibers in a state of complete relaxation while only those necessary to running are working."[4]

Running relaxed helps you in two big ways. You want your muscles to keep contracting forcefully over the long haul and keeping them loose makes this possible. Also, you want to keep getting as much oxygen as you can to your muscles, and relaxing your breathing achieves that.

If you come from the clenched fist, grit-your-teeth-school and need to be shown the logic of relaxed running, just go to the track and do this test. Run a lap and keep your arms and legs tight. Pretend rigor mortis is setting in. Clench your teeth and fists. Note how you feel and how much effort the run takes. Then run another lap at the same pace, this time keeping everything relaxed. Note how much easier the lap feels.

If you want to test your sprint speed, then do what Coach Winter had his athletes do. Mark off a thirty-yard zone on the track. Accelerate into the zone, so you are going your fastest when you get there. Have someone time you for the thirty yards. Sprint through the zone all-out, straining and pressing for every tenth of a second. Do that several times and average your time. Then sprint the zone at nine-tenths speed several times and average. Check the difference. You'll find you're significantly faster the second way.

Calming the Body

The reason for this has to do with biomechanics—how your muscles function best to move you over the ground. In running, the prime movers are your quadriceps (the muscles on the front of the upper leg) and your hamstrings (those on the back of the upper leg). Like other paired sets of muscle groups in your body, they work in tandem to produce a fluid motion. When your foot is on the ground and you are pushing off (the "drive phase" of your stride), your quads are contracting forcefully.

During this phase the antagonistic counterpart, the hamstrings, should be relaxed. When your foot leaves the ground and your leg swings forward (the "recovery phase"), your hamstrings are firing and your quads should be resting. Now, if this isn't the case, if you have some residual tightness in the muscle as it starts to contract again, it simply won't do its job as efficiently. The strength of the contraction is diminished, the energy cost is greater, the range of motion is lessened, and the chance of injury is increased.

You can see this clearly when you watch a runner who is tying up at the end of a race. He has a jerky motion. And if he's *really* tying up, he might even start to run in place! The natural action of his muscles is out of sync.

Keeping your breathing relaxed is just as important as keeping your muscles loose. If you'd like a demonstration of how important, just hold your breath, start running, and see how far you get.

When you get nervous, the muscles that assist the breathing action get tight. Muscles in your neck, rib cage and diaphragm constrict and cause you to breathe more shallowly. Shallow, rapid breathing upsets the natural intake of "good air" and output of "stale air," and correspondingly, it upsets the balance of oxygen and carbon dioxide in your blood. In the extreme, your constricted breathing upsets your inner ecosystem so much you get dizzy or nauseous, or you hyperventilate. And when you're racing and you want all the oxygen you can get, but you're getting less and less, it's panic time. You're "choking."

Relaxed breathing means deep, full belly-breaths, complete inhalations and exhalations. Tests have shown that one effect of relaxation is decreased oxygen consumption. For the distance runner this means he'll require less oxygen to run the same speed. He'll run more within himself and be less winded.

50

Learning how to calm your body is a matter of sensitizing yourself to your body. Many of the physical changes related to arousal creep up on you. You're very tight or winded before you know it. Staying in close touch with your body puts you at the top of the inverted - U curve, ready for peak performance and ready to head off any physiological tendency to go over the top. Learning how to do this is a skill much like other physical skills. You follow specific steps, and you acquire the skill through practice. Several effective relaxation techniques are being used by athletes today.

ACQUIRING THE SKILL

Around the turn of the century, Dr. Johannes Schultz of Germany developed a relaxation procedure he called "autogenic training." Using hypnosis to reduce the anxiety level in his patients, Schultz observed that the process of the body relaxing seemed to follow a pattern: First the arms and legs felt heavier, then they felt warmer, then the heart rate dropped; next the breathing relaxed, the midsection felt warmer, and then the forehead got cool. Schultz eventually taught his patients to elicit the relaxed feelings in these areas on their own.[5]

In the 1920s, Dr. Edmund Jacobson, a Chicago physician and physiologist, developed a similar procedure which focused on getting the skeletal muscles relaxed via a "triggered" response. "Progressive relaxation" he called it. Working with hyper-tense patients, Jacobson found it didn't help much to *tell* his patients to relax. Instead he found that if a patient flexed a specific muscle, held that tension, and then released it, the muscle relaxed a lot more than otherwise. And if a patient practiced this procedure with each muscle group, he would learn the sensation of relaxation so well that eventually he could put himself in that state quickly anywhere.[6]

More recently, Dr. Herbert Benson, associate professor of medicine at the Harvard Medical School, has done extensive tests to determine the exact physiological effects of various relaxation techniques, including hypnosis, progressive relaxation, autogenic training, and transcendental meditation. He found similarities in the physical response elicited by these techniques: a decrease in blood pressure and heart rate, a decrease in respiratory rate, an increase in Alpha waves (brain waves present in a person in the relaxed state), an oxygen consumption decrease (8 percent decrease when we sleep—20 percent after just three minutes of meditation), blood lactate decreases (acid in the blood stream, associated with anxiety and fatigue). Benson provided important scientific substantiation of the "Relaxation Response," our "natural and innate protective mechanism against 'overstress,' which allows us to turn off harmful bodily effects to encounter the effects of the fight-or-flight response."[7]

For several years I have used a form of progressive relaxation with the runners I coach. I like progressive relaxation for a number of reasons. It's easy to learn, it "takes" with everyone, it can be self-induced, there are no machines, it fits in nicely with other aspects of our training (stretching and mental rehearsal), it's straightforward and not perceived as weird, and it doesn't cost anything.

Many variations of Dr. Jacobson's procedure have evolved over the years. The cues and instructions I use are tailored to runners.

We use the relaxation routine in the stretching phase of our training session. Once or twice per week we tack on ten minutes of progressive relaxation to our stretching. I encourage the athletes to do additional practice at home.

The environment should be quiet and undisturbed, a place where you can get comfortable. We use our school's wrestling room where it is warm and padded. We go into the progressive relaxation routine after doing the "lying down" stretching exercises.

I encourage the runners to have a particular attitude about the routine. They are practicing something which will make them feel better and help their running. With regular practice they will develop a body sense for relaxed muscles and they'll be able to elicit that feeling before and during their running. Sometimes in doing the routine, getting relaxed will not come easily. Tensions may not go away completely. They needn't worry about that. They only have to maintain a passive attitude about the sensations they feel and the thoughts they think.

These are the cues I give as I lead them through the routine:

I. Lie on your back, arms at your sides, eyes closed. Roll your head around. Shake out your arms and hands. Jiggle your legs and feet. Stretch all over like a cat. Get thoroughly comfortable.

II. Now pay attention to your breathing. Breathe through your nose. Inhale slowly and deeply, hold at the top of the inhalation, then exhale slowly and completely, pause at the bottom, then inhale again. Each of these phases can take a three-count: Inhale—one and two and three, hold—one and two and three, exhale—one and two and three, pause—one and two and three. Feel yourself relaxing with each breath. Feel the regular flow of air in and out of your nose. Put your right hand on your belly. Inhale, the belly comes up; exhale, the belly comes down. Feel the good feeling of full, deep breaths. Feel the fatigue and tightness leaving each time you exhale. Feel the pure oxygen filling every part of your body.

III. Now you're going to raise your right leg about six inches off the ground. You're going to flex hard the entire leg, from toes to groin for about ten seconds. Tighten the leg and hold that tightness. Point your toes outward and feel the tightness in your foot and ankle. Then point your toes at your head and feel the calf flex. Hold the tension in your thigh and feel the tightness. Now release—let your leg drop. Jiggle it back and forth. Note the feeling of looseness. Feel the much-better feeling of relaxation and warmth. Feel the spontaneity and lightness in your legs. Repeat the same procedure with the left leg.

IV. Now you're going to raise both legs off the ground about six inches, and you're going to hold that for ten seconds, flexing your entire midsection. Flex your abdominal muscles, tighten your buttocks. Feel the tautness through the stomach. Hold that, study it. Now let go, let your legs drop. Take three long, deep breaths. Feel the opposite feeling of relaxation in the butt and stomach. Learn the feeling. Feel the glow of warmth in the midsection. Feel yourself centered.

V. Now direct your attention to your back. You're going to arch your back and tighten all along the spine from your neck to your tailbone, and you're going to hold that for ten seconds. Press

53

your head back and feel the tension. Arch up higher and feel the tightness in your back. Now let go. Feel the ease and comfort return. Feel the tension seep out. Roll from side to side and feel the relaxation getting greater.

VI. Now you're going to reach up and grab an imaginary bar hanging straight above your chest. Grab the bar, straighten your arms, and tighten them as hard as you can. Fists, wrists, forearms, biceps, triceps, shoulders. Hold on for dear life. Clench your fists. Feel the tightness through the arms. Study it. Now let them drop. Shake the arms. Feel the looseness. Enjoy the feeling. Feel the potential quickness and readiness there. Come race time, that's the way your arms will feel.

VII. Now focus on your chest, neck, and shoulders. You're going to do three things at once. Press your arms in at your sides to tighten your chest, arch your neck, and shrug your shoulders. Hold the flex for ten seconds. Tighten hard. Feel the tightness in your pectorals. Feel the tension in your neck and shoulders. Now let go. Feel the return of utter relaxation. Learn the feeling. Feel the pleasure of well-being. Soak in the warmth.

VIII. Now work on your face. You're going to make the most horrible grimace you can. Tighten all your facial muscles. Clench your teeth. Twist your mouth. Tighten your jaw. Wrinkle your forehead. Close your eyes tighter. Note the agitated emotional state that attends this. Now let go. Feel the tightness drain away. Feel your face muscles sag. Put your palms over your eyes and feel the warmth. Feel the relaxation spreading throughout, deeper and deeper.

IX. Scan your body for any areas of residual tightness. Relax them—tense, hold, then let go. Stretch all over like a cat. Feel the relaxed state of your body. Feel the suspended, weightless feeling. Tune in to your breathing. Long, effortless, full breaths. You are completely relaxed now. You'll remember this feeling. You'll be able to repeat this feeling before and during your race.

As you practice this relaxation routine. there are several guidelines to keep in mind.

1. Content

There is not just one correct way to do progressive relaxation. I've seen routines which start with the face and end with the feet. The main concept to follow is to progressively relax one area of the body after another. *The wording you use to go from exercise to exercise can be individualized.* You should develop your own set of instructions, the ones that work best for you. You can have a partner give you the instructions, as I do with my athletes. Or you can record your instructions, and then use the tape to lead you. Soon, however, you will know the instructions by heart and be able to proceed without any prompting.

2. A Cue Word

Practitioners often use a "cue-word" (or "code" or "mantra") during the relaxation routine. On each exhalation they repeat to themselves a word or phrase. Typically, this word has some suggestive power, such as "one" or "calm." Using a cue like this has two purposes. First, repeating the word focuses your thoughts on that word and away from worrisome thoughts. Second, the word can be used to get at stored memory. For example, to get yourself calmer on the starting line, repeat your cue, and it elicits the same response it did during the relaxation routine. With my athletes I explain this notion and have them practice using the word "one." Their using a cue is up to them; if they feel it helps them, they use it. They have it in their repertoire of mental training strategies.

3. Becoming Adept Using Progressive Relaxation

Just as you have goals for improving your workout times, you can have goals for improving your skill at relaxing. If you practice regularly and diligently over a period of months, you should see improvement that is just as real as workout times. For example, relatively soon after using the routine, you should be able to relax each area of the body without first having to contract the muscles there.

The next state of improvement is to relax the entire body without having to work on one area at a time. Along with this improvement you ought to be able to go to this thoroughly relaxed, full-body state faster, so that instead of a ten-minute process, you can achieve the state in a matter of seconds.

Also, instead of requiring a distraction-free environment, you will learn to attain this relaxed state anywhere—driving your car, standing in a line, typing a letter, running a workout.

If you practice everyday, you ought to achieve these stages within a month. The final stage is ongoing: You get better at relaxing in tense situations and maintaining your grace under pressure in big races.

4. Using a Log

By using a log you can hold yourself accountable for practicing the routine, and you can chart your improvements. Because most runners already use a running log, this amounts to one additional notation. See Chapter Seven.

5. Breathing

Doing this sport well has a lot to do with breathing properly, and yet this skill is often neglected. "Doing what comes naturally" is a skill in this case because many not only forget how to breathe in stressful situations, but have also forgotten how to breathe properly all the rest of the time. Many think proper breathing is heaving out the chest and sucking in the belly. (It's crude to let our bellies hang out!) One only has to look at a baby sleeping to see the correct, natural way to breathe. The belly rises on the inhalation, the belly goes down on the exhalation. Breathing just from the chest is shallow, incomplete breathing, whereas belly-breathing is full and deep.

Shallow breathing is a bad habit and the cause of all kinds of running problems, from "stitches" to anxiety. Use the relaxation routine to practice proper breathing.

6. Mental Rehearsal

Progressive relaxation is often used in conjunction with another training strategy, mental rehearsal. You "rehearse" the

56

race by watching it with your "mind's eye." Progressive relaxation normally is used right before in order to bring about a state conducive to quality mental rehearsal. More on this in Chapter Four.

7. "Heaviness"

This word is often used in progressive relaxation routines— "Feel the heaviness in your legs"—because it helps elicit further, deeper relaxation. But *heavy is the last thing runners want to feel.* So I rarely use the word in the procedure. Instead I use "light." It may not be as conducive to relaxation, but it's the feeling runners want.

8. Sleeping

Because you get so relaxed during progressive relaxation, you may fall asleep. Some psychologists say this is undesirable since you don't get the full benefits of the relaxation response and you aren't practicing to attain it during the wakeful state. They advise people to sit rather than lie down to prevent falling asleep. I'm not convinced falling asleep is undesirable. If one of my runners falls asleep, I figure he's had a late night and he could use a nap. Of course, another important use of progressive relaxation is to help an athlete get to sleep the night before the contest.

9. Before Workouts

Though the routine can help runners attain an optimal state for racing, it can also help them in workouts. I've seen runners come to practice dragging, and after fifteen minutes of progressive relaxation and mental rehearsal, they are rejuvenated and ready to attack the workout.

10. Muscle Soreness

I've found that athletes are so in tune with their bodies, they learn the routine very quickly. *One thing to anticipate with some*

57

runners following the first one or two sessions is a little muscle soreness. Progressive relaxation amounts to many isometric drills with muscles that may be unaccustomed to that kind of work.

ON-SITE

"They find they can relax just fine in a room away from the competition. But it's *out there* where they need it." Sports psychologist Dr. Rainer Martens has worked with several groups of top athletes from U.S. national teams. He knows that unless the athlete can apply his learning under pressure situations, it does him little good. And that is no easy task. "When you're standing at the top of a ninety-meter ramp preparing for a ski jump, that *is* cause for some natural worry, and that's when you need to stay relaxed."[8]

Transferring relaxation skills from the quiet of your room to the stadium is a challenge. Sports psychologists offer no quick solutions to this challenge. What they do emphasize is that mastery of the skills will take hard work and practice—diligent, regular, long-term practice.

With that priority clear, I'd like to offer several pieces of advice which may help once you arrive at the race site.

1. Scanning

Become adept at scanning your body for tight areas. Sweep your attention from area to area and take stock: feet and legs— "loose as a goose"; stride—arching through naturally and fully, not abbreviated; stomach, chest—hanging like loose meat; shoulders—dropped, relaxed, not raised; hands—loose, not fisted; and face—jowly, bouncy, not straining.

As you scan, if you find a tight area, flex, release, and shake out. Sometimes squeezing the area helps. Take a few deep breaths, exhaling slowly and completely. Invariably, you will loosen up.

2. Cue Word

If you use a cue word in your relaxation routine, the race site is the place to put it to work. Repeat the word to yourself. It will help trigger the same relaxation response with which it was connected during your off-site practice.

3. Breathing

Remember to check to make sure you are breathing properly—from the belly. Also, if you need something to take your mind off worrisome thoughts, plugging into your breathing is one of the best things, It's always in the here and now.

4. Nine-tenths

Keep in mind Coach Winter's advice. Whether you're sprinting at the beginning of the race, or at the end, or surging in the middle, remember—nine-tenths speed (or less). Don't press. Hold that little something back. Run within yourself.

5. Anticipate

In your past races, at what times did you notice tightening? When you first arrived and looked at your competition? The moment before you started your warm-up? The third quarter of the race? A steep hill on the course? If you can make such a connection, then anticipate, imagine yourself being the master of that moment, and when you get to that moment on race day, pay special attention to relaxing.

6. Imitate

Watch other runners who run very relaxed and imitate them. The power of the visual image is strong.

7. Attitude

Assume a nonjudgmental attitude. If you're feeling tight, attend to it, but don't worry about it. Worrying only aggravates the situation. Some days tightness may not go away at all. Keep disengaged emotionally. Maintain your dispassionate cool.

8. Bracing

Our discussion so far has been based on the assumption that in most cases when you're in competition, bringing your arousal to the optimal level will require backing up, relaxing yourself. *It is possible, however, that for some people on some days, what is needed is not backing up, but pumping up, psyching up, or as psychologists refer to it, "bracing."* You get to the race, and you feel lethargic and unenthused. On these days when you feel this way, you might be smart to consider not racing at all, but if you choose to, it's not so hard to get pumped up. Just employ tactics which are opposite to the relaxation routine. Clench your fists and teeth. Hyperventilate. Tell yourself this is the most important race of your life. And generally do all the things football players do on the sidelines right before the start of a game.

OTHER METHODS

You can develop the skill of calming your body in numerous ways. Progressive relaxation is one way. This chapter concludes with brief descriptions of some of the other techniques. Once you have an understanding of the various methods available, and have tried some of them, then you can make a sound decision about which is right for you. That, of course, is the bottom line in developing any training program, mental or physical: Do what works best for you.

Hypnosis

Unfortunately, the image hypnosis often conjures is the volunteer who is on stage in a trance and squawking like a chicken. In fact, hypnosis is a thoroughly respectable and conservative tool that is commonly employed in sports.

There are several forms of hypnosis. For example, a hypnotic state can be self-induced, or it can be induced by another. The induction process includes relaxing and focusing on one object so that your normal awareness of many externals drops. Your receptiveness to suggestions then increases. (Less than 10 percent of people are highly receptive to hypnosis). While in this state, if suggestions are given for you to become loose, your body may very well respond that way. "Post hypnotic" suggestions can also be given, such as, "When you see the starting line, you will relax."

Transcendental Meditation, Zen, Yoga

These are each forms of meditation, Eastern in origin. Meditation is somewhat different from the other relaxation practices mentioned in this chapter because it calms the body by working on the mental side; the mind is diverted from worries and then the body relaxes. There are many variations, but most meditative practices call for a quiet environment, a passive attitude, and the repeating of a word. Scientific evidence has largely verified the claims of Zen monks and yogis that meditation can enable one to control "involuntary" processes in the body, like heart rate and oxygen consumption.

Biofeedback

You can use machines to help you learn how to relax. If you are hooked up to an electromyograph, for example, you can watch a reading of your muscle tension. By seeing what is happening in your muscles as it happens, you get immediate feedback, and you can eventually learn the muscular feeling of relaxation, learn to control the graph, and learn to relax your muscles. You can also monitor your heart rate, your brain waves, and your skin temperature. Biofeedback training has been used with athletes for several years and has proved very effective. See Chapter Four.

Running

Running itself can be a way of calming the body. Physical exercise tends to release the static tension in the musculature (the same principle behind flexing and releasing in progressive relaxation). Also physical exercise tends to remove you from yourself. You don't sit and stew in your worries. Sports psychologist Dr. William Morgan refers to this phenomenon as the "Time-Out" effect. In his work at the University of Wisconsin, he has compared the relaxation which comes through running with other methods of relaxing.[9]

One runner once told me, "Once I start my warm-up, my nervousness goes away." The "Time-Out" effect has important relevance for runners. On occasion I have had my team run a couple of miles the first thing in the morning before a big, pressure race like the state meet. It helps burn off the jitters.

Ingesting Something

If you are having trouble calming your body, obviously there are things you can take which will induce relaxation—from drugs to alcohol to your own secret concoction. These are used at every level in sports. Certainly, they have helped many get a good night's sleep before competition. Understand that whenever you do use some outside agent to control arousal, you lose some control. And you don't want to be anesthetized for a race and lose the sharp edge of concentration.

Hot Baths, Whirlpool, Steamroom, Sauna, Massage, Analgesic Balm

Heat on the body, as well as massage, can also help bring about relaxation. I find a hot shower the morning of a race does wonders. Again, search around for what works best for you.

You can train your body to relax, and in turn, because of the mind-body connection, your relaxed body will help quiet your mind. This works . . . to an extent. If you are preparing for your race and you're working on relaxing the body only, while at the same time your mind is trying to flood your nervous system with signals of worry, then you're working at cross purposes, and your efforts may fall short. You have to work on both sides of the mind-body equation.

We took up the issue of calming the body first for a reason. It's relatively easy to relax progressively various parts of the body. When it comes to controlling thoughts, that's a more elusive matter. We're somewhat less self-conscious dealing with the body than we are with the mind. We're more at ease making assessments and prescriptions about the body, training it, almost as if it were someone else's. But when it comes to examining the mind . . . now that's closer to home. We identify more closely with the mind, and it's a little harder for us to be objective, to scrutinize it, to train it. Harder perhaps, but still well within our ability.

There are things you can do—definite, acquirable, step-by-step strategies—that will help you prepare your mind for peak performance. You can study the mental processes that occur during competition. You can quiet your thoughts and improve your powers of attention. And you can learn how to program your mind for successful races.

CHAPTER FOUR

Preparing the Mind

"When I hit the front I got a flash of compelling certainty. I didn't look over my shoulder, but I sensed someone coming up on me fast . . . I was already at full stretch. But I went into a sort of mental overdrive, and my subconscious mind took over completely—I've experienced it in races before, and I can't explain it."[1]

—John Walker

"There was no pain, only a great unity of movement and aim. The world seemed to stand still, or did not exist. The only reality was the next two hundred yards of track under my feet."[2]

—Roger Bannister

"I was for those minutes completely and utterly relaxed, unconcerned about the outcome, yet completely absorbed in what I was doing. I was in what has been described as a cocoon of concentration, absolutely involved, fully engaged in running. Not racing or winning but simply running. Everything was harmony and grace. Everything was pure. Effort had become effortless."[3]

—George Sheehan

Sometimes you can *see it*: Steve Prefontaine, his head cocked up at the track clock, absorbed in the battle against fleeting seconds; Lasse Viren, eyes intense, face impassive, a picture of concentration.

65

You have experienced it yourself. The moment of pure confidence and resolve. Controlled energy—like fusion in a nuclear reactor. Instinctive. Wide awake. Unlimited. Wordless. Magical.

What we have is a picture of the race-mind operating at its best. When we've experienced these moments, it's usually by accident. Wouldn't it be something if we could tap into this state *intentionally*! Is it possible to learn what brings about this heightened awareness, to practice it, then employ it in our races? How can we go about this?

The place to start is to learn a little about the key operating mechanism, the human brain.

MACHINERY OF THE MIND

To better understand the complex workings of the brain, metaphors have been used. The computer has been the most recent metaphor used, and the comparison is an especially applicable one. The brain can be seen as an information-processing system like the computer. The brain-computer model can help us understand the mind of the performing athlete.

Suppose you are in a race and winning with fifty yards to go. You are smiling and waving to your girlfriend in the stands. Just at that moment, another runner flies by you. What mental processes occur? Assuming you are paying *some* attention to the race, you'll hear and see the runner pass, and this sensory data will flash to your brain. There the data are changed to electrochemical impulses, the "language" of the nervous system. These data are received, assessed, and operated on by a mental program. This "program" is your pre-set intention for the activity of racing, electrochemical instructions saying—"In a race, you try to beat the other guy to the finish line."

This program is activated and your memory bank is searched for an appropriate bodily response. In this case, instructions for "Accelerate!" would be sought, and once found, signaled through the nervous system to your muscles.

When your leg muscles receive the signals, they'll respond . . . as best they can. If the muscle is not already too fatigued and if there is still sufficient oxygen for the muscles, then you may indeed accelerate.

This response is immediately monitored by a feedback system. Nerve impulses are sent back to the brain where they are assessed, used for possible "course correction," and stored in your memory.

This entire process happens in just milliseconds. You react "instinctively."

On the other hand, it could take you somewhat longer to react if you engage another function of your mental machine, your thinking. Perhaps conditions exist now in the race which conflict with your original intention. Perhaps you have a sore foot and speeding up would be unwise. Your thinking must be engaged to preempt or adapt the original program. Thinking needs to intervene when decisions or compromises must be made, or when new problems arise. (Of course, thinking can intervene anytime, for any reason, or no reason at all. You may have the thought, "Someone passed me! Now I won't win!" But it would hardly be much help.)

The quality of your response in a race, therefore, rests on four key things: (1) your *attentiveness* to the race; (2) the clearness of your *mental program*; (3) your *thinking*; and (4) the state of your musculature and your cardiovascular systems. The first three things are the object of our study in this chapter. First, we will look at how your *attention* and your *thinking* work and how they affect your racing. Then, just as a computer owner might do once he understands how his machine works, we will learn how to make effective *mental programs*.

(PAY) ATTENTION

"I recall watching a track meet at UCLA. The runners for the 440 were in their blocks waiting for the starting gun. The gun barked, and all the runners except one catapulted out of their blocks. The man nearest the gun got up, puzzled. He hadn't heard the gun go off. Concentrating on his form, on his strategy, he had failed to hear the gun go off. His preoccupation with the interior self was so complete he neglected to heed the one aspect of conscious awareness critical to his goal. He had directed the physical being so completely he had turned off hearing."[4]

Barbara B. Brown in *Supermind: The Ultimate Energy*

It is the Moscow Olympics 800 meter final. The field is stringing through the first 400 meters. Pre-race favorite Sebastian Coe is trailing, staying out of traffic. On the backstretch of the final lap, Nikolay Kirov makes his move. Steve Ovett barrels after him. Coe notices, moves outside listlessly. One second . . . two seconds go by. Soon Coe is flying after the leaders. He gains ground, passes the struggling Kirov, but there is no more time or distance. Coe ends up second. Later, in embarrassment and disgust, he tells reporters, "I simply didn't respond when the break was made."[5]

Attention means your awareness of the various stimuli in your environment. Each of your five senses plays an important role in your awareness, with vision assuming a lead role—80 percent of the stimuli you attend to comes through your sight.

What sights, sounds, odors, tastes, and touches are you aware of at this moment? Only a few? Many? Think of your attention control as a kind of sophisticated lamp, having several functions. You can shine your attention in various *directions*. For example, you can direct it at external things, like this book page or the ticking of a clock. Or you can attend to internal things like your breathing. A second major function is scope: you can change the *width* of the beam your attention casts. You can send off a narrow beam and attend to very few things, as you would when concentrating on a putt in golf. Or you can send off a wide beam and take in many things at once, as you do when you drive a car down a busy city street.

Attention in athletics is vitally important. The master of attention will consistently perform well because he can shut out the churning of his stomach and the screaming fans, and control his attention so he is always in the right place at the right time and his response is automatic.

Attention can be a problem for distance racers. Some of the difficulties were stated in Chapter Two. Attention can go astray because of the length and repetitiveness of distance running. Attention can be distracted because of excessive worry or fatigue. And because runners have a tendency toward an internal focus, their attention can be less flexible. Poor awareness of what is happening in a race is common, especially in inexperienced racers, and invariably it prevents quality performance.

A distance runner, therefore, ought to have a very clear notion, first, of just *what things he should pay attention to* during the race. The race entails several important actualities, internal and external ones, to which he must attend. What are the key points of attention?

First, you must attend to several *internal bodily sensations*. Already we hear protest: "My body? Are you kidding? I just want to forget my body in a race! I get more out of myself. Why pay attention to the body?" Some of the research of sports psychologist Dr. William Morgan offers illumination on this question.

In the 1975 testing of elite runners mentioned earlier, Dr. Morgan asked his subjects about their "coping strategy" in races. He found an interesting similarity in their answers. "The elite . . . runners constantly monitor bodily signals of respiration, temperature, heaviness in the calves and thighs, abdominal sensations . . ." One runner gave this observation: "As the run progresses, I remind myself to drink a lot of fluid . . .I also pay a lot of attention to my feet as I run. I used to get blisters a lot, and I think you can prevent that by paying attention—maybe removing your socks if you're wearing them. Also I *read* my calves and thighs and I pay a lot of attention to my breathing." Morgan concluded that one thing that characterized the psychological strategy of the elite racers was that they carefully attended to, or "associated" with their bodies.[6]

Morgan was surprised by this because he had tested another group of runners and had found something different. Working with a group of ordinary joggers, he learned that, by and large, these runners *tried not* to attend to the body. Instead, they would attend to externals like their splits, or more commonly, their thoughts. They would divert themselves with mind games like building an imaginary house. Not attending to body feedback Morgan called "dissociation." Interestingly, Morgan found that dissociation was actually an effective strategy for this group. The dissociators could stay on the treadmill 30 percent longer than the control group.

How does one explain this sharp difference in coping styles? Morgan suggested three good reasons why the better runners used an associative style. First, they are in better physical condition and are much more familiar with discomfort from their training, so they can "afford" to attend to the body. The pain just isn't that bothersome. Second, the better runners learn to read the body well because

69

this enables them to avoid problems like blisters or dehydration during the race. Dissociation is potentially dangerous. One is reminded of Jimmy Carter and the many other joggers who get into trouble and overheat in a race simply because they haven't heeded the body's natural signals.

. Third, the better runners associate because it helps them conserve energy and maintain a physiological steady state. Only by being closely in touch with the body can they know exactly how hard they can push themselves. It is interesting to note that not only did the elite group use far less of their oxygen capacity compared to the joggers (suggesting a more efficient use of energy), but also they were far better at giving descriptions of their fatigue levels which accurately reflected their actual physical state.

Ultimately, to get the most out of your body in a race, you need to pay attention to your body. Here are some of the key particulars:

> *Legs and arms:* Read your legs and arms in order to maintain a loose, light feeling and fend off tightness and heaviness.
>
> *Warning signals:* Monitor a variety of signals—stitch, blister, rubbing, foot soreness—and appraise the seriousness.
>
> *Rhythm:* Attend to your running rhythm. Fluidity and efficient form must be maintained, especially in the later stages of fatigue.
>
> *Temperature:* Stay aware of your body temperature and your state of dehydration.
>
> *Breathing:* Strive to control your breathing.
>
> *Pace:* Carefully attend to your pace and the amount of exertion you are putting out.
>
> *Pain:* Related to pace, pay attention to the discomfort of windedness, muscular fatigue, and tightness. Pain is the ultimate race reality. By attending to it, you can keep it under control and strike that delicate balance—to run as fast as possible and still keep back from the brink of fatigue and tightness which, if crossed, will ruin your race.

A personal story here will punctuate the importance of attending to the body. In college, I noticed that my racing was always much improved for a while right after returning to school from a vacation. I would have a very good race-feeling for a few weeks; then this feeling would gradually ebb away. The difference seemed to be in the training I did away from the team compared to the training I did with the team at school. Somehow I was preparing myself better away from the team. But how? It took me a while to analyze it. There was the possibility that my own workouts were more sensible than the high-volume school workouts. Also there was a confidence aspect, the fact that I was "winning" my solo workouts, rather than "losing" workouts at school. But there was something else, and it had to do with attention.

During the school workouts I would be in a group of four to eight, and invariably I would be content to draft along behind the leaders, trying for relaxation, and attending only to contact. This way I was pulled through some great workouts. But by attending almost exclusively to contact, was I missing out on something? After a few weeks of these group workouts, I would be much less aware of my body during the run. By not keeping familiar with the discomfort, by not practicing holding the body in that "delicate balance," that important sense would fade. I was able to regain this awareness only when I included more solo workouts in my training.

So much for the internal things to which you must attend! (Of course, you attend to your *thoughts* too, an important issue, which we'll take up shortly in the next section.) How about *external* actualities? To what things outside of yourself should you attend?

The *competition* is usually a main concern. At times you might be way ahead in a race, or way behind, or in some way separated so that paying attention to the competition is unnecessary. But these times are rare. Usually you have others close to you in a race. And really, you want it that way. The competition helps you get the most out of yourself. You use your opponents to draw out your best race effort.

If you are vigilant, you pay attention to who your opponents are, where they are during the race, and what they are doing. You pay strict attention to your position among others on the track or course, attempting to position yourself advantageously and stay out of traffic. If you are alert, you rarely get cut off or boxed in; you are in the right place at the right time. If you are following, your attention is riveted on contact. You focus on a shoulder, relax, and

71

drift along (staying out of the wind can conserve as much as 10 percent of your energy). You strive to keep within "striking distance," knowing that once contact is broken, your job becomes more difficult. If you are leading, you check your competition when you can, in glances, on turns. You listen. You try to sense where your opponents are and what they will do. Whether you are following or leading, if you are really alert to the competition, you will react quickly to moves—even sensing a move before it is made and striking first.

When you are battling an opponent, you are putting all kinds of information through your computer. How did the rival take that last hill? How did he respond to that last surge? What is his breathing like now? His foot strike? All this attention helps to answer an important question: How much does the other runner have left?

Have you ever seen this happen? Two racers are playing "cat and mouse" in a race, watching each other closely, preoccupied. They completely disregard another runner, who ends up beating them both. You must be judicious about your attention to the competition. There are other opponents to consider and considerations other than competition. Flexibility of attention is essential.

A second external actuality is the *race course*. Where does the course go? How far to the finish? How far to the next split or water station? How far until the final kick is made? Simple things, but often neglected. Partly a matter of planning, but also a matter of paying attention. In high school indoor track, the freshmen two mile is a source of great comic relief. Consider a dozen or more freshmen running a twenty-lap race. Many are on different laps. The official lap counter has given up. Few of the runners are paying attention to what lap they are on. Many have no idea how far they have left to go.

On the roads and the cross-country courses, if you are alert, you are processing information about each upcoming turn and hill and chuckhole. You use each part of the course to your advantage. In a recent national cross-country championship Henry Rono suddenly found himself on a narrowing path getting crowded away from the leaders by a mass of runners. He quickly jumped up onto the stone wall bordering the path and ran along on it to catch up. That's paying attention!

Another external priority is a temporal consideration—*race splits*. In our state track meet, split-times for the distance races are read aloud clearly. Yet each year at least half of the two milers, nervous and distracted, end up going out much faster than their capabilities allow, and their races suffer.

You must be attentive and make sure you hear splits. That way you can adjust your "cruise control" if you need to. Split information is an important supplement to your body's sensing of pace. And, it can be a major reliant. Gauging your race on what the competition will do is less reliable than the constant of time.

Splits, the race course, the competition, the body itself . . . these are the main realities in a race. But are these the only things you need to be aware of? Aren't there many other things that you could notice? Here a Zen master's advice is helpful: "Expect nothing. Be ready for anything." In the '81 New York Marathon a spectator broke out of the crowd and plunged into the lead group of runners. He actually got to one runner and tried to stuff money into the runner's jersey before he was straight-armed and knocked away. Here the alertness of the runners averted a potentially race-damaging accident.

Pay attention to the high-priority items already mentioned, but at the same time, stay ready for anything. What you try for is a wider, open-focus attention. Practitioners of Zen refer to this as "the senses touching everything."

This moves us from the realm of *what* we should attend to in a race, to the realm of *how* our attention should operate.

How will the direction and width of your attention change through the race? There are several key relationships to remember here. The shorter and more rapidly changing the race, the wider and more external attention tends to be. Such is the case in an 800 meter race with a bunched field constantly rearranging. Your main concern is traffic and position and staying alert to rapid shifts. On the other hand, the longer and less changing the race, the narrower and more internal your focus is likely to be. In a marathon, whole segments of time might pass with you focused only on a thought and little else. Another key relationship: The beginning and the end of a race will tend to elicit a wider, outer attention because these parts

73

are usually more changing. The middle of a race will tend to bring about a narrower, inner focus. So in this way the race itself often dictates the direction and width of attention.

Direction and width of attention will naturally and spontaneously change and move during the race. Flexibility and appropriateness of attention are important. You don't want to be so preoccupied with contact, that you can't hear what your body is saying. You don't want to be looking at your stopwatch as you run down a street of chuckholes.

How does anxiety affect attention? Increased anxiety tends to cause your attention to suffer. Both the control of your attention and the spontaneity of your reactions deteriorate. Your attention becomes clumsy and inappropriate.

How much thinking should intervene in your attention during a race? How does thinking affect your running? These issues we take up next.

I THINK, THEREFORE I AM . . .
I Think

"Should I be doing something at a given moment? Should I make my move now? Should I sit and kick?"[7]

—Jim Stintzi

"Bill [Rodgers] has often said that his marathon strategy is to hang on, feel out the competition, let them run themselves into the ground and take over the lead saying to himself, 'Look out. Once I grab the lead I'm going to really be running well and you're going to have to kill yourself to catch me.' This is a *very* positive statement."[8]

—Ron Wayne interview with Bill Rodgers

"Look how smooth he runs. Did you see his relaxed expression? That's the key to his strength. It's Zen . . . The idea is to clear your mind of everything and to let your body function naturally, undisturbed by thoughts. That's something most Americans and foreigners can't understand."[9]

—Coach Kiyoski Nakamura talking about Toshihiko Seko

74

Thinking is closely related to attention, yet it is also quite distinct. Like the rest of the animal kingdom, we humans can attend to things, and prompted by our various biological needs, like any animal, we can move toward or away from these things. But unlike animals, we humans can also *think*.

This wasn't always the case. At some point in the distant past, before we had language and before our brain began to triple in size, we couldn't think. Our species evolved, and as luck and natural selection would have it, we learned to talk to each other, and perhaps more important, we learned to talk to ourselves—what the scientists call our "symbol-producing capacity."

This new capacity to think enabled us to improve our living conditions and advance in dramatic ways. But the fact that our mental hospitals are full suggests this capacity to think comes not without cost to us. Pascal, the 17th century philosopher, spoke this caution about thinking: "Man holds an inward-talk with himself alone, which it behooves him to regulate well."

The thinking human can cause problems for himself. Through his self-talk, he can create imaginary dangers. A runner can turn a three-mile race between Smith High School and Jones High School into a terrifying event. He thinks about the upcoming race, thinks about every past bad race, thinks about every possible bad happening. He replays them, takes them apart, reconstructs them, gets emotional, and redefines the whole experience. A remade "fact" emerges: "I might (and probably will) run horribly in this race—and that's a fate worse than death."

Once, I had a runner work himself into such a panic before a race he couldn't bring himself to the starting line. Rather than face anyone, he ran four miles back home.

Two years ago I had a fine miler who qualified for our state meet. He breezed through his preliminary heat Friday, running with the self-assurance he had shown all spring. He won the heat going away in one of the fastest times of the season. The mile finals were late in the afternoon Saturday. Instead of bringing him over to the meet with the rest of our team, I let him come over to the stadium later. That was a mistake. He sat alone in his dorm room for three hours, and I can only imagine the thinking that went on. By the time he got to the starting line for his race, he was a different runner from the day before, having convinced himself he could not win.

75

Two thousand years ago another philosopher, the Roman Epictetus, stated the problem this way: "Men are disturbed not by things, but by the views which they take of them."

There is a surprising amount of divergent thinking about thinking and athletic performance. Sports psychologists, coaches, and gurus disagree about the role of conscious thought in performance. This section presents some of the notions which are commonly put forth and debated.

Most agree that thinking is necessary in certain *strategic* situations during performance. Situations will arise in your race when you have to adjust to the unexpected; re-strategize due to changing conditions; analyze various options and formulate solutions, compute, look ahead, recall things, make decisions. These situations require thinking.

Perhaps you hear a split and realize you are off pace. You decide to pick it up gradually and calculate that if you speed up five seconds per mile, you'll be right on pace after three miles. Or perhaps your competition starts kicking with a half-mile left. Instinctively, you want to go with him, but then you think. "Is it wise to start my kick this far out?"

Alberto Salazar is an excellent problem-solver in his races. In the '82 New York Marathon he developed a bothersome stitch. He reasoned that it was only a matter of time before the stitch would go away. Until then, he didn't want a faster pace. So he dropped off the leader, Rudolfo Gomez, about ten yards. He reasoned that by doing this, Gomez would not be inclined to force the pace. The plan worked. No increase in pace. Eventually the stitch subsided. Later in the race, when it came time for the final kick against Gomez, Salazar decided on the best possible moment. As they entered Central Park, they crossed a gravel area where the lead press truck sent up a thick cloud of dust . . . It was at this moment of confusion and distraction Salazar chose to strike. Again, the tactic worked.

We find another area of general agreement about three basic relationships regarding thought and performance: (1) The longer the event, the more opportunity you have to think. (2) The more unpredictable and changeful the event, the more necessity you have to think. (3) The more you have practiced, learned, and programmed your performance, the less necessity you have to think.

When we move beyond these basic notions about thought, we see much disagreement. Some insist that thinking is the downfall of the athlete. After all, why does a football team take a timeout right before the opposing team's kicker tries a field total? To get the kicker *thinking*, of course. And if a sprinter has to think about starting when he hears the gun fire, instead of just reacting to the sound, he will have already lost the race.

The proponents for clearing the mind of all thought during a competition put forth a persuasive case. Tim Gallwey, author of *The Inner Game of Tennis*:

> "When a player is 'on his game,' he's not thinking about how, when, or even where to hit the ball. He's not trying to hit the ball, and after the shot he doesn't think about how badly or how well he made contact. The ball seems to get hit through an automatic process which doesn't require thought. There may be an awareness of the sight, sound, and feel of the ball, and even of the tactical situation, but the player just seems to *know* without thinking what to do."[10]

Dr. Robert Singer, sports psychologist at Florida State University:

> "Ideally . . . in competition the body performs with little need for deliberate cognitive intervention. Focus should be on the minimal number of most relevant cues. Information derived during or after the performance should be monitored. Thought processes need to be quieted but directed toward positive outcomes."[11]

D. T. Suzuki, in the foreword to *Zen in the Art of Archery:*

> "As soon as we reflect, deliberate, and conceptualize, the original unconsciousness is lost and a thought interferes . . . The arrow is off the string but does not fly straight to the target, nor does the target stand where it is. Calculation, which is miscalculation, sets in."[12]

The idea here is that thinking only serves to slow down and prejudice your body's spontaneous, pre-programmed response. Our

77

body functions perfectly well without help from conscious thought. The biomechanics of the running motion is mind-boggling in its complexity, and yet the body carries it off with ease. If you had to think every stride—"Now place the foot. Now roll forward off all five toes. Now flex the ankle and calf."—the act of running would be impossibly complex.

And it is important to understand the unthinking nature in which we perform any act well. Consider a time when you were absorbed in an activity, say typing. You are processing a tremendous amount of minute stimuli. Thoughts rarely intrude. You are "in the moment." This absorbed state results in your best work. The finished product will show it.

An interesting study was done examining the thoughts of distance runners during a long race. It gives validity to the idea that little conscious thought is done or is needed during the performance. Sports psychologist Dr. Mike Sacks and a team of assistants questioned ten ultramarathoners periodically during a one-hundred-mile race. These researchers posed the question:"What have you been thinking about during the last lap?" Many responses indicate the runners were attending to and thinking about the body ("That little muscle in my left leg around the knee hurts.") and the race ("I know how far I have gone, how far to go, and roughly what my pace is.").

Yet much of the time, the investigators also heard comments like this: "Well, not really anything," and "I'm not thinking about much." The comments suggested a blank state of mind, similar to the state of mind you might have while driving your car on a long trip. Mike Sacks concluded: "These runners were spending hours focused on nothing, simulating a meditative process in which any ideas, feelings, or images simply run through the mind and fade from view."[13]

These observations do ring true. How much conscious thinking can you remember doing in your best races?

Zen masters may insist you must keep your mind thoughtless, like the calm surface of a pond, but until you become a Zen master, the waters of the mind before and during competition invariably are more like the inside of a churning washing machine than a still pond. Face it, you have a lot of time during a distance race and you are naturally going to have positive and negative thoughts. So it behooves us to examine the content of these thoughts. What effect does the content of your thoughts have on your race?

Many sports psychologists have studied this question. In 1965 a Soviet researcher, A. T. Puni, found that an athlete's use of oxygen, and subsequently his performance, improved when his mental state was filled with positive thoughts and emotions.[14] William Morgan, in more recent research, found that subjects pedalling on a stationary bicycle, when *told* the bike's resistance had intensified (the resistance being controlled from outside the subject's cubicle by the researchers), experienced greater bodily stress—as shown by higher pulse rate and other indicators—*even though the resistance had not actually been increased.* In other testing, researchers have found this phenomenon works the other way too: Subjects told the resistance was lessening would manifest less bodily stress, even if there had been no actual change in resistance.[15]

This research suggests how potent our thinking can be, and it gives credence to the conventional wisdom about positive thinking. Undoubtedly, many athletes find positive thinking beneficial to their performance and essential to their mental preparation. It may well be that when Bill Rodgers says to himself, "You're going to have to kill yourselves to catch me," there is a corresponding, positive physical effect.

Some runners entertain inspirational thoughts. Others recall Biblical passages. Coach Bud Winter has athletes repeat very positive sayings to themselves in their pre-race preparation to instill a powerful mental set. Sports psychologist Dr. Jerry Lynch uses the same technique. He refers to it as "positive self-affirmation." "When repeated often enough, they (the positive phrases) become part of your belief system."[16]

The "power of positive thinking" school of thought obviously is sharply different from the "still your thoughts" school. Consequently, there is ongoing debate. Tim Gallwey sees positive thinking as only a little less disruptive than negative thinking. Any thinking during the contest, Gallwey feels, engages your ego, causes you to start judging, and results in dividing your attention. He sees positive thinking as just self-criticism in disguise.

What actually happens when you tell yourself "I'm feeling

great! Let's go for it!'"? Does that generate inner imperatives which then cause you to start pressing? Or does it improve your performance?

What sense can we finally make, then, of all the pondering about this pair of mental processes, attention and thinking? Two main prescriptions emerge from this discussion.

(1) You ought to have some understanding of the mental processes going on during performance. You should have some awareness of the distinction between attention and thought as well as the interaction between the two. And you should become aware of your own style of attending and thinking in races.

(2) These mental processes will be subject to much change during performance. Typically, you will experience an ebb and flow of your attention and thought. The main point is for you to exert some control over this. You ought to *plan* how you will *attend* to the race and how you will *think* it, just as you would plan how to run it.

One of the best explanations of this second point I've seen is Don Kardong's analysis of marathoning strategy. It is a strategy which got him fourth place in the Montreal Olympics. "I have a theory on marathon running, where a rational approach is so important. During the first ten miles of the race, I try to disassociate myself from what I'm doing. I talk, joke, and daydream in ways that remove me from the race. But after ten miles, my consciousness re-enters the picture, and concentration begins. From that point on, the problem is concentration, and the feeling is one of acute association with the task at hand. I switch from automatic pilot to manual control, and through the last part of the race, I pick off those people who have over-associated, i.e., who have tried to concentrate from the start."[17]

Kardong's strategy was to break the race into segments and to plan how to use his head in each segment. In this way he could better regulate his energy and maximize it. The strategy worked beautifully for him. What's more important, however, is that it illustrates a very sound principle of race preparation. Figure *4-1* suggests a similar methodology. (See pages 82–83.)

ENHANCING YOUR ATTENTION AND THINKING—
PRACTICE EXERCISES

What can be done in practice to prepare you and help you achieve an optimal mental state in your race? A number of very effective methods are now being used by psychologists, coaches and athletes. The following exercises represent some of the most productive of a mixed bag of techniques. Some will aid attention, some have to do with thoughts. Some are to be done after progressive relaxation. Some are race-simulations and are done during running practice.

(1) Attention Span

Sometimes in a race you want to "lock onto" one particular stimulus. It may be an external one, such as an opponent's shoulder, or an internal one, like the feeling of looseness in your legs. You want to coast for a while, conserve energy, and recharge your battery. Doing this entails the ability to hold a single attentional focus. You can practice this skill in an easy way. Simply choose some object, any object, and see how long you can watch it. This is a universal meditative practice. By contemplating the single object and holding your attention on only that, you quiet your mind and strengthen your attention.

This should be done in conjunction with progressive relaxation. After your body is thoroughly relaxed, you go into the exercise. Your watching of the object may last two minutes or twenty minutes, depending on your motivation, your proficiency, and the available time. Don't be overly concerned with how long you can hold your attention. The only goal is regular practice. Try to keep your mind thought-less during this exercise, but if and when thoughts do intrude, that is perfectly O.K. Don't try to keep out thoughts. Recognize them, consider them briefly, and let them pass out of your mind as you return your attention to the object. Remain cool, calm, detached.

In watching the object, try to stay fascinated by it. The specific object you use can have some suggestive importance to you, though it doesn't have to. Here are a few possibilities:

81

Figure 4-1

HOW THE DISTANCE RACE INFLUENCES ATTENTION, THOUGHT AND ENERGY

STAGES OF THE RACE	RACE DEMANDS	ATTENTION	THOUGHT	EMOTIONAL ENERGY
STAGE 1: FIRST 1/8 TO 1/4 OF RACE. (THE START)	STAYING OUT OF TRAFFIC; SETTING A PACE; SETTLING INTO POSITION; INITIATING YOUR PLAN; GAINING RELAXATION.	WIDER ATTENTION NEEDED; MORE EXTERNAL ATTENTION.	SOME THOUGHT NEEDED; MATCHING EXISTING CONDITIONS TO YOUR RACE PLAN.	SOME ENERGY DEPLETED.
STAGE 2: NEXT 1/4 OF RACE. (MIDDLE OF RACE)	RELAXATION; SMOOTH FORM; EXECUTING RACE PLAN INSOFAR AS POSITION, PACE, MOVES.	NARROWER ATTENTION IS POSSIBLE; MORE INTERNAL ATTENTION.	LITTLE THOUGHT NECESSARY.	IDEALLY, ENERGY STORED AND "CHARGED" AND USED JUDICIOUSLY TO RESPOND TO PROBLEMS .

STAGE 3: THIRD 1/4 OF RACE (MIDDLE OF RACE)	SAME. BE AWARE OF NECESSARY CHANGES IN PLAN DUE TO THE UNEXPECTED; RELAXATION UNDER PAIN.	NARROWER ATTENTION IS POSSIBLE; MORE INTERNAL ATTENTION.	LITTLE THOUGHT NECESSARY, EXCEPT TO ADJUST TO THE UNEXPECTED.	IDEALLY, ENERGY STORED AND "CHARGED."
STAGE 4: LAST 1/8 TO 1/4 OF RACE. (THE FINISH)	"END GAME." SETTING UP FOR KICK; DEALING WITH PAIN; DECISION-MAKING.	WIDER ATTENTION NEEDED; MORE EXTERNAL ATTENTION.	MORE THOUGHT NEEDED; STRATEGIZING, DECISION-MAKING.	RELEASE AND USE UP ALL REMAINING ENERGY.

Plan how you will put your attention, thought, and energy to optimal use.

(A relationship to remember: The shorter the distance race, the more rapidly changing it can be, and therefore, the more *reacting* you will have to do and the wider and more external your attention will have to be—and the less time you will have for conscious thought.)

—A stopwatch set at the time you want to hit in your race. (When Rick Riley was trying to set the national high school two-mile record back in 1966, he wrote down "8:48" and posted it at home where he could see it regularly. He eventually did set the record. His time: 8:48.3.)

—A photo of the track, the stadium, the road, or the cross-country course where you will run.

—A photo of a running hero you would like to emulate.

—An award, or a photo of it, which you would like to win.

—Your own breathing can be the object of your attention.

—A word or phrase repeated can also be the object of your attention (in Eastern religions, a "mantra"). This could be any word. The word "one" is often used because it has some suggestive power.

(2) Wide Attention

Sometimes, especially at the beginning or end of a race, or in any shorter distance race, or in any race situation where there are more changes and distractions occurring, a wide field of attention is desirable. You will want to be awake and alert to your environment. At the same time, you will want to be discriminating, filtering out irrelevant stimuli. Additionally, you'll want to maintain relaxed concentration. This is a skill like other skills, and it can be developed through practice. One way is to use a simulation drill which stresses this attentional skill.

This simulation drill, as well as the next two, works best in a team or club setting, where there is a group of runners and a coach present. During a workout session the coach asks the group to do a hard run of a prescribed distance and pace. He tells them to stay alert, relaxed, and goal-oriented. While they are doing this run, a second group is instructed to run alongside and harass them, throwing elbows and shoving. One "planted" runner may take a wrong turn midway. Another plant might try to upset the prescribed pace. Splits are read right as "spectators" on the sidelines are yelling and screaming. Other "spectators" might insult them or give wrong directions. The harassed runners must keep their cool and stick to their goal.

The drill is great for developing the mental set to be alert and to handle distractions. It desensitizes runners to upsetting occurrences. Lefty Driesell, University of Maryland basketball coach, would play a tape of screaming fans as his team practiced. He claimed it prepared them for unfriendly crowds.

(3) Attention to Contact

Racers soon learn that maintaining contact is a very important skill. Simulation drills are an effective way to teach this skill. This particular exercise gets at maintaining contact, running in traffic, and responding to surges.

A group of runners (four to eight seems to work best) run a fartlek together. A runner initiates a surge without warning, and the rest of the group must respond and keep contact no matter how long or fast the surge is (that is up to the leader). Everyone takes turns surging during this fartlek, but there should be no set order.

(4) Attention to Various Actualities

A coach can use another drill to reinforce and direct attention to various other actualities, such as form, breathing, and relaxed concentration. The runners work out in an infield area where the coach can watch each individual and make himself heard. While the runners do a fartlek in this area, the coach directs them from one object of attention to another. He might, for example, call out, *"Feel* yourself rolling off all five toes," or, *"Feel* yourself using your *whole* leg." These kinds of cues reinforce correct form. The coach might give the instruction to *"Pay attention* to your breaththing,"* or, *"Feel* the looseness in your arms and legs," or even "Check out the discomfort you feel and see how *unemotional* you can be about it." One real value of these cues is that they are much more concrete and useful to the runner than the standard, vague cues he usually hears: "Relax! Concentrate!"

One excellent addition can be incorporated in this drill. Have the runner give a rating of how he is feeling as he works on each of the various instructions. For example, let's say he is attending to his breathing. As he runs by the coach, he gives a rating of his breathing—anywhere from 1, a labored, panicked breathing, to 10, a totally relaxed "within yourself" breathing. What is happening, as the 4's and 5's become 7's and 8's, is that the runner is learning *inductively* the feeling of relaxed, controlled breathing.

(5) Biofeedback and Attention

For a number of years, people have used biofeedback to gain control over a variety of physical processes. Now biofeedback is being used to teach the control of mental processes also. A fascinating study was done at the University of Illinois in 1979 with twenty-two top runners. It was under the direction of Dr. Les Fehmi of the Princeton Biofeedback Clinic. The athletes went through a series of mental exercises aimed at teaching them attentional control. Hooked up to sensors, they could monitor their own brain wave patterns, among other things. According to the study, the athletes learned how to broaden their attention, thereby releasing psychic tension, and attaining a state of *effortlessness . . . at will.*[18] This work is continuing. The prospects are exciting!

(6) Positive Thinking

Two important techniques you can include in your repertoire of mental preparations for racing have to do with the self-talk you do. Your thoughts, both during a competition and especially before, as we have shown, can have a big impact on your performance. Repeating positive statements to yourself has been found to be a potent technique for strengthening self-image and developing a positive mental set for performance. You can see it as "priming the pump." After a period of "simply" speaking positive statements about yourself (some researchers say at least three weeks), you can actually effect real changes in your psychological make-up and hence, your behavior.

This is an exercise which should follow progressive relaxation. You are much more open to suggestion when you are relaxed. Silently or aloud, in present tense, you repeat your chosen phrases at least four times each. Devise phrases that work for you. Here are some examples:

"I am a stronger runner every day."
"I am cool, calm, and collected at the race."
"I feel loose, quick, and light in my running."
"I enjoy the challenge of the race. I enjoy taking risks."
"I have great reserves of strength."
"I feel sharp and alert."
"I am resolute in my goals for the race."

(7) Creative Worrying

This technique is based on the notion that you are naturally going to have some worries about your race and the best way of dealing with that is to set aside a specific time and place where you can entertain all your worries and then shelve them. With this technique you think through each worrisome aspect of the pre-race period and the race. Picture yourself worrying like crazy. Don't picture poor performance, just yourself worrying. Choose your own set of scenarios. Here are some examples:

—worries about your training and about how you will feel on race day . . .
—worries about the crowd, your parents, your friends, your coach . . .
—worries about the pressure, about *having* to do well . . .
—worries about the competition . . .
—worries about the course or the weather conditions . . .

Stay with each situation until you feel your anxiety drop. Worry systematically and intensely and . . . humorously. Make your scenarios crazy and outrageous. This helps you internalize the silliness of anxiety. Do creative worrying well in advance of race-day. And then leave it.

This helpful technique works for a number of reasons. Most people strain to keep their minds off worrying, but in fact, end up worrying for days. This mental "house cleaning" accepts worrying as natural and lets you deal with it briefly and efficiently. Creative worrying also helps you crystallize your worries instead of being beset by vaguely diffused worries. Creative worrying is a way of desensitizing yourself to worries.

87

PROGRAMMING YOUR COMPUTER

Jack Nicklaus calls it "going to the movies."

Before the Mexico Olympics 400-meter final, Lee Evans sees every stride he will take in the race, feels each one. He watches himself win. Which he eventually does, in world record time.

Bruce Jenner has a hurdle in the middle of his living room. Each evening he practices trailing his leg over it, visualizing his race. He spends hours mentally rehearsing every one of the ten events he will do in the Montreal Olympics.

Dwight Stones stands at the top of his approach and watches the high jump bar. His head nods a few times, his arms and right knee come up, his body twists. He sees his entire approach and take-off. Now he is ready to jump.

Craig Virgin is running sprints across the finish line of a cross-country course in Madrid. He is fixing in his mind the picture of the kick he will use the next day to win the World Championships.

Olympic gold medalist Jean Claude Killy stands with a stopwatch in his hand. Eyes closed, he mentally skis the entire race course, visualizing every turn and rough spot. His rehearsal time is remarkably close to his eventual race time.

Before the '80 Olympic Trials Marathon, Tony Sandoval carefully pictures all 26 miles. He watches himself getting splits, taking the lead, surging. He watches himself breaking the tape . . . an image which would come true.

These champion athletes all hit on something that worked. They were tapping into a very powerful function of the brain—its capacity to be *programmed* to produce desired behavior through a visualized rehearsal of that behavior.

At one time or another we've all stumbled upon this powerful capacity. I recall a time in high school reading a book about one of my running idols, Peter Snell. I was wrapped up in the book, saw myself in the races, envisioned myself setting world records. I read the entire book in one evening. It happened that I had a race the next afternoon. I went to the race with all the images of Snell's powerful running still in my head, and I demolished my previous personal best time.

88

Most of us catch glimpses of this "hidden talent" in the same way—by accident. But there are those who use this natural function of the brain with more intention and method and have seen stunning results. Steve DeVore, author of *Sybervision: Muscle Memory Programming for Every Sport*, relates a story about trying out his theories on mental rehearsal at the bowling alley. His all-time high score in bowling was only 163. While watching professional bowlers on TV one day, he decided to put to use the visuals in front of him. He gave his complete attention to the bowlers. He relaxed and watched and concentrated. He saw strike after strike. Then he went to the bowling alley where he bowled nine straight strikes in his first game and eight strikes in his second, before the "groove" began to fade. But by then he knew he was on to something.[19]

Why does mental rehearsal work? There are four ways this question is usually answered.

First, like any other kind of rehearsal, mental rehearsal is extra practice which makes you more familiar with how you will perform. Mental rehearsal is a simulated run-through where you can try things out. You can be creative. You can rehearse troublesome parts of your performance and allay any doubts you may have.

Second, mental rehearsal works because it has an actual neurological effect on your body. As you sit and mentally rehearse your race, calling up images of it, you are activating your brain's cortex. This activity can be detected in a brain-wave test. Simultaneously, neural signals are fired off to the muscle associated with running, causing small amounts of muscle contraction. It is a kind of "testing the circuits." These contractions are subtle, not enough to cause any gross movement. Yet this activity also can be detected at the muscle site, through a muscle-graph test.

Actually, you can prove this to yourself with a simple experiment. Take a length of string and tie a small weight to the end. Hold it over the center of the diagram (Figure 4-2). (See page 90.)

Keep your elbow on the table to stabilize your arm. Now visualize the string and weight swinging along the north-south line. Soon it will begin to move along this line, even though you are not trying to move your arm at all. By "just" visualizing you are producing muscular contractions. Practice visualizing the string and weight stopping at the vortex and then moving along the east-west line.

Figure 4-2

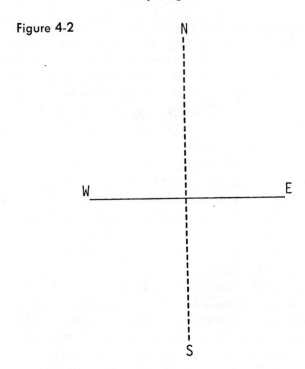

Scientists have long known that images and words can both have physical effects in the body. Apparently, the nervous system recognizes little qualitative difference between an action that you visualize and one that you can actually carry out. The neurological system is activated in both cases.

In the third explanation we enlist our computer model again. In your computer's memory banks you have many programs of behaviors. There is a reason to believe, in fact, that *everything* we see and do is imprinted. Imprinted, but not necessarily recallable. (There is the story of the bricklayer who, under hypnosis, could describe every single detail of a brick he laid in a wall ten years back. The man had put in about two thousand similar bricks on that day. The indication was that under hypnosis he could recall the individual details of any one of them!) You have many similar mental programs for your races, but unless you have raced perfectly every time, some of these programs will be effective ones, some not so effective.

How can you be sure in a race that you will retrieve from your memory the right model for all the right physical and mental race-behaviors—the perfect model? Two things which help are watching perfect races and visualizing perfect races. In effect, what you are doing is rematching, refreshing, rewriting, and refining a high-quality race program. At race time you have a better chance to retrieve this newly recreated and reactivated program. Instead of calling up terrific races 5 percent of the time, you can increase it to 10 percent, and then 20 percent, and so on.

Finally, mental rehearsal is often compared to both hypnosis and dreaming. Like hypnosis, with mental rehearsal you are wide awake the whole time, but focused within yourself. You are in a more relaxed and suggestible state. And like hypnosis, mental rehearsal cannot produce any performance skills you don't already have or any feats you are physically incapable of. What hypnosis and rehearsal can do is strengthen self-belief, aid relaxation, and help you make the most of what you do have.

Mental rehearsal is similar to dreaming because it seems to tap into the unconscious and draw on similar powerful illusions. The main difference is that with mental rehearsal you are in control of this state.

The history of the study of mental rehearsal goes back to the late 1800s when it was debated whether gymnastic movements could be learned through a visualized, nonphysical kind of practice.

In recent times, one famous study tested students' ability to shoot free-throws. The students were all tested on Day 1 to ascertain their scoring percentage, and then they were divided into three groups. Group A practiced shooting free-throws everyday. Group B did no practice whatsoever. Group C spent twenty minutes each day imagining themselves shooting free-throws and making the shots. They had no other "practice." After twenty days the groups were tested again. Group B showed no improvement; Group A improved 24 percent through their practice. Interestingly, Group C, having practiced "only" in their imaginations, improved almost as much—23 percent.[20]

One additional finding of note here: Within the mental rehearsal group, it was found that a student's improvement corresponded to his ability to evoke a clear and detailed mental picture.

For example, one student had trouble picturing himself bouncing the ball; the ball would stick to the floor! His improvement was negligible. Other subjects were able not only to *see* their whole action very clearly, but were also able to *feel* the ball and *hear* it bounce. These subjects improved the most!

In recent years, many sports psychologists have developed various forms of mental rehearsal to use in their work with individual athletes and teams. For example, Richard Suinn of Colorado State University has used what he calls "visuo-motor behavior rehearsal" (VMBR) with excellent results. In his initial testing of his procedure with the university ski team, Suinn divided the team into two equal groups. One group added VMBR to their ski training, the other group trained as usual. The VMBR group improved so much they ended up ruining the study. The team's head coach was so impressed by the VMBR group that he chose to race them in the meets and not the skiers from the other group. His team won both the men's and women's division championships and the conference overall title.[21]

How can distance runners put mental rehearsal to use? What follows is an illustration of the mental rehearsal I have found successful with my teams. Initially, I lead the group through the mental rehearsal—I talk them through the steps. This would come before the running workout and after a session of stretching and progressive relaxation. Keep in mind this is a *general* example of rehearsal. In an actual rehearsal of your own, you would want to include all the various specifics of your upcoming race.

I. See yourself completing your warm-up before the race. You have done your easy running and you have stretched out well. You have done some high-quality build-ups. You feel loose and quick-legged. You feel confident, alert, and eager. You take note of your competition, get good luck wishes from your friends. You call up images of your race plan. You take your position on the starting line. You feel nervous but also composed and ready—as you await the start.

II. The gun fires. You get a quick, smoothly accelerating start. You move into position, expending some energy, letting it out judiciously. You are alert, watchful. You make note of your initial split time. You are on the outside, staying out of traffic nicely, away from the jostling. You identify your main competitors. You are where you want to be. You feel fluid. You are settling into an efficient pace now. The temporary breathlessness—the lag in your oxygen transport—is leaving. You have distance to go, but you feel strong and know you have great reserves!

III. Your plan today is to maintain contact with a particular opponent. You follow him just off his shoulder, feeling very relaxed. Your contact is good. You feel very within yourself. Your opponent seems to be pressing. You come through your next split. It's a little slow; you feel your opponent lagging, and you realize you ought to move on. You surge, letting out energy, but feeling strong. You move up to another runner, assess his pace, and fall into his wake.

IV. You let him pull you for a while and you try to relax. The pace is challenging. At times you feel winded and fatigued. You make note of it, reminding yourself it's only temporary. Your split times are fine, and you feel good about that. You attend to the course, readying yourself for each part, the hill, the sharp turn. At one point, you step in a hole, and you stumble for a few strides. You regain your composure, settle back into pace. You try to maintain a dispassionate cool and bide your time.

V. Later in the race your opponent is applying some pressure. He surges. You tempo up to maintain contact. You definitely feel the fatigue, the breathlessness, some tightness. You get control of it. This is the challenge of the race to which you want to respond. You hang on, knowing that soon, with 880 yards left, you can go hard . . .

VI. You check your form, feel yourself lifting, pulling through. You feel an alertness, a clarity. You are charging your battery. You are in just the right position. You summon up your reserves, ready for the final push. When you hit your mark, you surge hard, and you gain some yardage right away. You feel power and speed. Also great discomfort—which you struggle to control. You feel yourself sustaining. You see the finish, the spectators. Shouts tell you someone is coming back at you. You dig down one more time and drive through the finish.

VII. You lean over catching your breath. You feel the satisfaction of competing well, running a good time. You see yourself satisfied and pleased as you start your cool-down.

This rehearsal is a simple procedure. Designed with high school runners in mind, it is fairly quick and easy, structured and relevant. After I coach the group the first couple of times, giving them cues, they can then go on to mentally rehearse by themselves. I do it this way for two reasons. First, I find beginners need to feel very sure of just how to proceed with the rehearsal. Second, this way I feel more assured that the rehearsal training actually gets done. As soon as possible, I have them doing their own creations, which will obviously be much more relevant and powerful. (Other methods are to have a friend lead you through the rehearsal or to put your own on tape.)

There are several guiding principles for mental rehearsal as well as applications. Here are a few of them.

1) In order to picture a race clearly and especially to picture high-quality racing, you need something on which to draw; you need to have been exposed to images of quality racing. To meet this need, you can watch films. More and more films of the elite racers are being marketed. Color films are best. Photos can also serve the same purpose. And obviously, whenever possible, watch top racing in person. Be aware—this is not casual viewing. This is paying close attention, being *absorbed* in the images.

2) It is often recommended you do the rehearsal twenty-four to forty-eight hours before your race (for instance, on a Thursday night before a Saturday race). This way, if you have any uncertainties about the race, you can put them to rest early. Normally, one rehearsal per week suffices, though you could practice it more frequently. It would not be good to use up emotional energy by rehearsing the night before the race. Reserve that night for resting and "de-psyching," doing things unrelated to running.

3) Mental rehearsal always begins with the relaxation procedure. Your body should be thoroughly relaxed, loose, and warm. Your mind quiet, but alert and open to suggestions. Your eyes should be closed, your breathing deep and regular.

4) You should run whole sequences of the race, if not the entire race. You can also include the warm-up and the warm-down. The idea is to get a holistic feel for the race, and not just snapshots of it. The amount of time you take to rehearse the race can vary. It need not be longer than the actual duration of your race; it can be shorter. Experiment. Try regular speed and slow motion. Try the Killy approach and use a stopwatch.

5) As you visualize your race, you may choose to *watch* yourself if you want a more detached, outsider's point of view. Or you may choose to actually *be* yourself in your "movie" if you desire a more intimate point of view. Some sports psychologists distinguish between these two techniques, calling the first "imagery" and the latter, "rehearsal." Either method is acceptable. Again, try both to see which works best.

6) Outside of visualizing your upcoming race, there are three additional options. You can experiment with these: Picture one of your past races—the best race you ever ran; picture yourself in the Olympic Games running your greatest race ever; picture yourself as one of your running idols in a race.

7) One absolutely essential principle is that your visualization be as rich in detail as possible: the starter's gun, the timers' watches, the other runners, the color of the sky and the race course and your uniform, the sounds of breathing, feet hitting, crowd cheering, and splits being called. Also odors: the smell of sweat, of analgesic balm.

Tactile sensations: the feeling in your stomach, the feeling of your footstrike, of the sweat on your face, of your jersey moving. Even tastes can be imagined: the water during the race, the oranges or yogurt afterwards. The richer your picture, the better. Athletes are most often limited, not by their lack of physical skills, but by their lack of imagination and their inability to imitate.

8) During your rehearsal it is important not only to picture yourself running brilliantly, but also to picture yourself assuming all the right race attitudes. Here are some attitudes you can see yourself projecting: relaxation, spontaneity, perseverance, alertness, acceptance, patience, "disinterested interest," determination. More on this topic in Chapter Five.

95

9) Mental rehearsal should consist of images of very positive, successful race behavior. However, you may also put to good use images of problems arising in the race and your handling each problem effectively. It is sound practice to entertain a few mishaps and surprises so that you can desensitize yourself to them and envision solutions. Getting overly nervous before a race, arriving too late for a warm-up, losing a shoe during the race, stumbling and falling down, dealing with a sudden rainstorm—various mishaps can be visualized. You will deal more effectively with the race problems because you will already have a program of successful emotional and physical response.

10) Computer information can be called up by giving a particular "code" to the computer to get "into" the information bank. In a similar way, codes are sometimes used in mental rehearsal. Some sport psychologists feel you can retrieve desired behavior more reliably by using codes while you rehearse and then using the same codes later during your performance. For example, during his mental rehearsal, a runner might say the word "easy" as he pictures a difficult part of his race. Later in the race when he says this word to himself, it can function as a kind of post-hypnotic suggestion and help him retrieve the appropriate feelings of relaxation, control, and perseverance. Word codes like this are commonly used; however, other kinds have been developed. Steve DeVore recommends the use of specific colors and eye shifts to elicit certain memories. Recent brain research is suggesting that codes, like call numbers for the books in a library, can greatly facilitate retrieval.

11) You might try using background music to enhance your suggestive state during your rehearsal. For example, the "Chariots of Fire" theme (which Dave Moorcroft actually used while preparing for his world record in 1982) may work at an emotional level to inspire greater confidence and will.

12) You can use mental rehearsal as a substitute for running when you are unable to run. During an injury period you can use rehearsal to stimulate and keep your "muscle memory." There is the example of a Soviet athlete who had been lying in a hospital bed for two years with a broken back. When doctors finally removed his bandages, they expected to see a flaccid, atrophied body. Instead,

they saw the muscle definition of a well-conditioned athlete! The patient explained that he had spent every day imagining putting himself through a strenuous regimen of running, weightlifting, and wrestling.

Visualization also might help you combat illness and injury. At Dr. Carl Simonton's famous cancer treatment center in Fort Worth, Texas, patients are taught to picture their healthy cells destroying the cancer cells. Recovery results at the clinic, as well as other current research are confirming the efficacy of "mind-assisted healing."

13) You can put mental rehearsal to good use after your races also. The same day, while the images and sensations of your race are still fresh in your mind, mentally play back the very best parts of your race. Only the best parts—there are always *some*. This practice is another way to instill the feeling of quality race behavior.

14) If you are having trouble visualizing your race (as you may, especially at first), here is a simple exercise you might try. Watch some object for a while—a desk light, your hand, a book page, a tree. Then close your eyes and see how long you can retain that image in front of you. Practice.

"Body Rehearsal" or Race Simulation

Boxers incorporate "shadow boxing" in their training. Can you practice your mental rehearsal while you are out running? Certainly, and there are several good variations on this theme, although most psychologists would hesitate to classify them under "mental rehearsal." Psychologist Tom Tutko, for example, advocates the use of "body rehearsal." The athlete swings his bat or his tennis racket or his golf club with his eyes closed, while he visualizes the perfect swing and attends to the feeling of the perfect motion. It enables him to gain a better "muscle sense."

I would hesitate having my runners run around with their eyes closed. However, they can make use of rehearsal and imagination in other ways. I prefer to classify these practices as race-simulations. Here are a few examples.

1) Your running workout can simulate the actual race in many

ways—the strategy you will employ, the effort you will have to exert, and so on. University of Oregon Coach Bill Dellinger has Alberto Salazar go out on a long run and loop back to the track every four miles to blast a 3/4-mile surge. Sebastian Coe finishes most of his workouts with a hard sprint to simulate the response he invariably must make in his races.

2) You can also pretend you are on the course where you will race. Visualize each part of the race, how it will be. Work on the troublesome parts and see yourself coping effectively. Create an imaginary opponent. What must you do in practice if you will be racing against a good kicker? What must you do if you will be racing a good hill runner?

3) Some helpful forms of "over-simulation," which pose conditions over and above what you will have to deal with in your race, can have a callousing effect. Benji Durden trains in Georgia with full sweats on so he can handle any hot weather racing. East German marathoner Waldemar Cierpinski incorporated thirty to thirty-five mile runs in his training for the '76 and '80 Olympics. Coming *down* to the marathon distance is a nice situation to be in.

4) Your imagination can be very active on a training run. You can put your imaginings to good use. Here are several "mind-games" that can be helpful and fun, can aid your running form, self-image, or just help get you through the last few miles of a long run.

—Pretend you are en route to winning an Olympic Gold.
—Pretend you are your favorite running idol.
—Pretend you are demonstrating "perfect racing" for some younger runners.
—Pretend you are running some information back through enemy lines. Civilization as we know it depends on you.
—Pretend you are the Zen master of running.
—Pretend there is a car towing you along.

In this chapter we have discussed three mental processes that figure prominently in athletic performance—attention, thinking, and imagination. We have looked briefly at how these processes function, and we have noted various applications and practices which make for their optimal use. In other words, how this extraordinary machine, your race-mind, works—and how you can make the best of it. Will this learning result in the kind of perfect races suggested at the beginning of this chapter? It will help. But there is something more involved.

In the next chapter we turn our attention from the machine to the operator of the machine. For the perfect running of the machine requires more than just knowledge of mechanics and methodology. The perfect running of the machine requires a certain kind of operator with certain attributes and a certain relationship to his endeavor.

CHAPTER FIVE

Gumption

"If you're going to repair a motorcycle, an adequate supply of gumption is the first and most important tool."[1]

Robert Pirsig

Pirsig's modern classic *Zen and the Art of Motorcycle Maintenance* is full of common sense about ordinary pursuits with broad applications. He says a lot that can be applied to distance racing, especially when he talks about gumption.

If you look up this old-fashioned word "gumption," you'll find several definitions. In one dictionary—"enterprise, initiative." In another—"courage, aggressiveness." For Pirsig, gumption has to do with a person's enthusiasm, his "reservoir of good spirits." It is the inner stuff that pushes the motorcycle mechanic toward the right solutions to repair problems—and the same stuff that drives us all toward success.

Finding solutions to the problems of racing well has to be at least as complicated and frustrating as motorcycle maintenance, maybe more. There are the injuries, the psych-outs, the fatigue, the boredom, the misinformation, the ways to let yourself off the hook, and countless other traps. I've muddled through dozens. A healthy supply of gumption is needed.

"If you haven't got it," Pirsig observes, "there's no way the cycle will get fixed. But if you *have* got it and know how to keep it, there's absolutely no way in the whole world that motorcycle can *keep* from getting fixed. It's bound to happen."[2]

The same way with running. If you're a runner who has gumption, you're bound to race well. If you have gumption, you take risks, you assert yourself. You've got enthusiasm. You're persistent. You maintain your confidence. You may be the most inept athlete on the block. You may incur injury and loss and stare at your running program as a frustrated mechanic stares at the parts of his broken-down motorcycle. But if you can hold onto your gumption, there's no way you won't eventually race well.

Consider the story of Dan. High school freshmen runners are often skinny, weak, and uncoordinated, but Dan took this to the extreme. I feared for him on windy days. Seeing his lack of physical attributes, I wasn't expecting much. He ran just under thirteen minutes for two miles his first year.

Two years went by, and despite his lack of success, Dan stayed out for the team. He'd been injury-prone and he was still emaciated. Somehow he kept his enthusiasm, kept working hard, ran a 5:20 mile in track season—a considerable improvement which I failed to notice—and put in another thousand-mile summer.

By the middle of his senior year, Dan's running had me and all his teammates paying attention. He ran 15:33 for three miles, 9:44 for two miles, and became one of the top runners in our school. The next year Dan ran 15:19 in the 5000 meter and placed third in his college conference. Dan's abundance of gumption rolled over his limitations and made possible his uncanny progress.

But gumption isn't something you either have or you don't. Your gumption level isn't fixed. Like an "emotional battery," it can be run down or charged up depending on what you do and how you think.

Consider the story of another runner of mine. Chris had little spark initially, but when a series of circumstances finally coaxed the spark to life, his transformation was brilliant. Tall and lean, with a fluid stride, quick turnover—Chris had all the makings of a fine runner. But something was missing. He'd get to the hard part of a race, where you have to move into the unknown in order to improve, and would back off. He'd keep his effortless stride, but he never engaged with the race. "Chris isn't a competitor," was the consensus.

At the end of his junior year in track, Chris ran a 4:31 mile, running alone in a slow heat. A large improvement, but it had little effect on him. Cross-country season found him still sleepwalking through races. "I knew it was there," Chris said later, "I knew I was on the edge, but I didn't have the confidence."

Fortunately, several circumstances converged to push him over the edge. In Chris's senior year another runner transferred to our school who wasn't as talented as Chris, but was a harder worker. Chris was soon number two. Then a younger teammate rose and began to push for Chris's spot. That jolted Chris; he trained harder, and got himself in great shape. A spark. At the same time he started to realize that if he didn't get going, there would be no college track scholarship. He'd been expecting to get one—his brother and his two older friends had gotten scholarships. In February Chris tagged along behind his teammate and ran a 4:25 mile, beating two of the better runners in the state. Another spark.

Then came The Breakthrough Race. In an even-paced, "setup" mile, Chris out-sprinted his teammates and blasted to a 4:18. His inhibitions fell away, and from that point on everything clicked. He ran 4:16 a few weeks later. The next week he ran 4:13 on Friday and 4:12 on Saturday and placed in our State Championships.

Your emotional battery is a sensitive device. A good workout, an encouraging word from a friend, or an unexpected win can deliver a disproportionately large charge of energy. On your next run your stride quickens, you're taller and lighter. A poor race, a piece of bad advice, or a minor injury can leave you slumped and sulking. Many things affect your emotional energy level, and this level, in turn, affects your running.

Here's the point: *You* be the controller of your emotional battery. Your energy level is subject to many influences, but it is not at the mercy of them. *You* monitor your gumption level. *You* make sense of the things influencing it. *You* recharge it when needed. *You* marshall all the sources of gumption.

What things can you do to charge your emotional battery and keep it charged? The considerations fall into two categories. The first category includes the *external* circumstances affecting you— the things you do and the things done to you, the happenings that garner energy and those that deplete it. The second category includes the *internals*—how you think, your attitudes and habits of mind, those that enable and those that disable.

This chapter examines some of these considerations. It is a

chapter of observations and practical advice about circumventing traps and building gumption.

WORKOUTS

"Did you hear about the workout I did last week? Twenty quarters in 50! Felt great! Am I *ready*!"

This remark says two things about runners and their workouts. One is that workouts provide prime material for a favorite pastime—the Tall Tale. (Workouts that are aged are even better. In a year this runner's 50-second quarters will have improved mysteriously to 20 × 440 in 48.) The other suggestion is the very real psychological power workouts have for runners.

Workouts give daily verification of our runner-ness. Workout time has a certain momentous quality. We get preoccupied with them. On top of actually *doing* the workouts, we plan them, record them, compare them, tell stories about them. We invariably attach more importance to workouts than is logical.

A great set of quarters puts us on top of the world. A sluggish, aborted training run throws us into depression. Our gumption level has a lot to do with how our training is going. And given this fact, one clear aim stands out: Do everything possible to make workouts psychological boosts rather than busts.

Volumes have been written explaining training programs and citing the physical effects. I won't add to that. Instead, I'd like to talk about the emotional effects workouts have on runners and what we can do in training to save and build emotional energy.

Make your rest days rest days

It may be strange to start a discussion about workouts with the topic of rest, but the fact is, there's no other training principle more important. First, understand that your rest days—days when you run easily or when you don't run at all—perform a vital function. Physiologists tell us the rest period between bouts of hard exercise is the time when muscle fiber repairs itself and the body adapts to increased stress. The body must be given recovery time. Second, understand the emotional factor. Hard workouts take emotional energy. (Hopefully, you'll get energy *from* workouts too, but this

104

equation is not a simple one.) You need the recovery day or days to recharge your emotional battery.

Here's where many runners go wrong. Typical "rest" day: 1) long run, 2) bounding drills, 3) stretching, 4) weight lifting, 5) swimming. They wonder why they never feel fresh! Nine of ten serious runners overtrain. They don't schedule enough rest days or they run too hard on easy days.

Craig Virgin observes, "More gold medals are lost in workouts than won in workouts."[3] Successful runners eventually learn the "secrets" to quality running: consistency, smarter work (not necessarily harder work), and rest.

Be vigilant

There are hundreds of training mistakes, culprits that can lay waste to your gumption. Missing sleep and trying to train hard, running long on a real hot day, risking injury running on a canted surface, coming to a big race feeling flat from too much speedwork, coming to an altitude race without acclimating first, doing a workout and being uncertain of its value, doing one designed for someone else. Head these culprits off with careful, thorough planning. Use foresight. Anticipate. Work to eliminate worry, confusion, and risk from your training.

See improvement in your workouts

Too obvious? You'd be surprised how many runners and coaches neglect it. Whole teams are running quarters at seventy seconds at the start of the season—and still doing quarters at seventy at the end. The picture can just as easily look like this: February 1, 12 × 440 at 73; March 1, 12 × 440 at 71; April 1, 12 × 440 at 69, May 1, 12 × 440 at 67. Seeing your workout times getting better is the single, most important gumption-producer you can derive from training. Plan your training so it provides you with clear signs of your improvement.

To do this, set up long-range and intermediate goals for particular workouts. Be aware your body adapts slowly to increased stress, so you will rarely see nice, linear improvement. You'll have plateaus and even setbacks. The idea is to plan occasional "marker" workouts—ones that, because of their similarity (four workouts of 12 × 440 during the season, for instance), will be indicators of progress. If you're smart, you wait to run a "marker" workout until you *know* it will show something positive. Before you run 12 × 440 again, wait until you know you can improve your average. In this way, you get regular injections of confidence.

There's another worthwhile workout, and this is the type author-runner Hal Higdon recently referred to as the Great Workout. Every once in a while you have days when you feel absolutely great. Smart runners capitalize on these special days. An awesome workout gives an awesome psychological boost. Coe runs his 6 × 880 in 1:52, Byers his 20 × 440 at 55. Higdon quotes Frank Shorter: "You get done and you say to yourself 'I'm ready.' " And Katherine Switzer: "They give you perspective, confidence, and a *sense of destiny*."[4]

Put variety and flexibility in your training schedule

Being consistent and regular in your training is an imperative for runners. ("Live like a clock," Villanova coach Jumbo Elliott advised.) But this principle must be carefully integrated with two other imperatives—variety and flexibility.

Running is a thoroughly repetitious activity, but it needn't be boring. Variety, a healthy stimulant to the nervous system, should be an integral part of any good program. Arrange a variety of training options. Vary your training sites. Have various running partners. Try running at different times of the day. Experiment with dozens of different types of work. Even within any one track workout there are countless options. Keep your training interesting—and your gumption high—through variety.

Runners get imprisoned by their own training schedules. "I *have* to do fifteen miles today so that I hit seventy-five for the week." Or you'll hear, "I've planned to do this set of quarters and today is the *only* day." The speaker doesn't seem to care that he has the flu coming on or the wind is gusting twenty miles an hour. This kind of rigid thinking invariably leads to staleness, injury, sickness, and loss of gumption.

Be flexible and keep an open mind about your schedule. Always keep this question before you—"Is this the *right* workout for *me* on *this* day?"

RACES

Good training gives runners a steady and convenient infusion of gumption. A series of good workouts has a powerful, cumulative effect. But of the many external influences on a runner's energy level, workouts rank number two in sheer power. Nothing helps a runner's confidence like a good race.

Racing, after all, is the object of the sport. Serious runners train to race. Races give a real and unambiguous evaluation of performance, a certified time, an official place. A rival beaten, or a personal record, stands as irrefutable proof of your success in your sport that day. The result is a healthy dose of confidence.

What considerations can we make to help insure confidence-building races?

"Set up" your races

Once the gun goes off, there are many things over which you have little control: What will your competition do? What will the leader's pace be? Whi will surge when? What will the race course be like and the weather? The smart racer tries to control as many race-factors as he can.

Set up conditions to your best advantage. Pick your race carefully, look for the distance, the course, the competition, and the day which will be best for you. Learn all you can about the race and your competition. Know your opponents' strategies, have your own figured out. Arrange for partners to help you through the race. Perhaps a friend can be a "rabbit" and help set the right pace. (The rabbit is a ubiquitous sight in world-class races today. The elite use them to run their best times, why shouldn't the rest of us?) Once in the race, follow through on your plans and make sure you get in the right place at the right time.

Setting up your races this way greatly increases your chances of hitting race goals.

Set up your races for improvement

When Jim Ryun was a high school sophomore, he started the track season running the mile in 4:48 and finished in June running 4:07. Booming along on gumption, he broke four minutes the next year and made the Olympic team.

Your improvement probably will be somewhat more gradual than Ryun's. The main thing is to *plan* for race improvement the same way you do for workout improvement. The same principles apply. If the mile run is your top priority, give yourself time between each mile race. Run 880's and two-mile races until you know you're ready to improve your mile time. In this way you arrange to get the important emotional lift that comes from seeing your race times drop.

Sometimes improvement halts, physical or mental "barriers" go up, and frustration sets in. Then it is time for patience and for planning the race that will get you through the sticking point. Plan for the Breakthrough Race—you can "make your own breaks."

Don't underestimate the power of a single race. In the earlier story about Chris, he improved only a few seconds, but his image of himself as an athlete was revamped on the spot. I once coached a runner who saw himself as a "five-minute miler." Try as he might, he couldn't break 5:00. His senior year he ran five consecutive races between 5:00 and 5:03. In his sixth race he ran 5:02. I called out, "4:59! Great race!" He was ecstatic. From that point on, he improved steadily.

It's O.K. to win

It feels good to win. Search for races where you have a chance to win and make use of this prime source of gumption.

Impossible, you say? The fields are too large, the competition is too tough? Perhaps. But I suspect that with a little study, you may find something. It may be a tiny, first-year fun run in Timbuktu. You don't even have to win outright. Maybe you win the age 35–39 male schoolteacher division—but you Win, and that makes a big difference.

Monitor your gumption during the race

Successful racing has a lot to do with your ability to get emotional energy during the race, sustain it, and build it. Several important axioms figure into the picture here. Your position in a race, for example, influences your energy. Leading a race is ego-boosting and empowering. It can also be nerve-wracking, taking the responsibility of pace-setting, trying to break down your competition, and trying not to get jumped from behind. When you follow, you lose control of the pace and give up the limelight, but you also have the more comfortable feeling of drafting and the strategic potential of surprising the leader. So understand there is an energy trade-off with leading and following.

Understand too the energizing value of maintaining contact with others. Unless you're leading and breaking away from others, your place should be right off someone's shoulder. There, you don't use emotional energy setting the pace, and you don't use it up paying attention to your pain because you're paying attention to contact instead (although you should monitor your discomfort regularly).

Learn to grab opportunities in races. Catch your opponent sleeping. Get five yards at a water stop. Follow a straighter line on a curve.

And what do you do when mishaps occur? You get tripped, for example, and you fall to the track. When you get back up, you have several options. You can feel sorry for yourself and let your gumption drain away. Or you can accept it and maintain your relaxed concentration. You can even see it as a challenge. The choice is yours.

The game is how to tame pain

If you've ever run down the last backstretch of a race, dead tired, your muscles tight with lactic acid, your rival trying to pass you and the wind gusting in your face, then you know the feeling. Or have you ever run down a road with an opponent, working each other over with surges for miles, only to face a killer hill at the finish? Then you know it. Races are painful. And to a large extent, how well you do in a race is dependent on how much pain you can tolerate.

How much pain you can deal with is closely related to your emotional energy level. So it's worth considering the things you might do and the attitudes you might have which enhance this relationship.

First, understand the subjective nature of pain. "It always seems that your best races didn't involve too much pain,"[5] observes John Gregorek.

109

Also, understand how training and lifestyle influence your response to discomfort. Oregon Coach Bill Dellinger advocates the inclusion of "callousing" workouts in training. If you're going to put up with pain in the race, you have to get used to it in training. Some advocates go further. Some say that to be a truly great distance racer, a stoical lifestyle must be adopted. A too-easy lifestyle, geared to seeking comforts, makes you soft, they say. When you're in the last mile of a marathon with two other runners right on your shoulder, you had better be hungry, better be used to discomfort. This is the point Kenny Moore makes about Henry Rono. "[Living conditions in Kenya] develop a realism, a clarity of judgment about such things as pain and effort, that is difficult for Westerners to share. As a distance runner, Rono has no illusions, which is good because . . . it is our illusion that we can go no faster, that holds us back."[6]

Once you're in the race, what do you *do* about the pain? The best advice here seems to be—recognize it, accept it, and welcome it because it represents the real challenge of the race. "Embrace it," Perry Cerutty, the great Australian coach advised.

One final consideration. Give yourself *time* between races. Schedule your races carefully. Make sure the next time you "go to the well," the well is full. (One indictment of American school running is that runners race too often.) Derek Clayton used to say he needed six months between marathons to forget the pain of the last few miles. Nothing is gained by racing when you're not emotionally recharged. Wait until the feeling of freshness and spontaneity returns.

Learn to cope with bad workouts and bad races

You've planned one more good long run before your next race. You get halfway through it, and your legs start to wobble and your breathing starts to labor. You struggle back home, feeling miserable, and your reservoir of good spirits drains. Don't let it! Act quickly and reason with yourself. Understand you can't have good workouts or good races every time. Your body doesn't work that way. You are bound to have bad days. They're your body's way of telling you it needs more rest. Don't fight these days. Cut back your workout or stop altogether. Race another time, or if you race, accept it for what it is—a bad day.

110

Also look at the positive things you did in the race. Maybe the first half was fine, maybe your kick was better. Maybe everything was horrible except for *one* thing. Keep that one thing in mind. Later, evaluate what went wrong. Coolly analyze the race. Learn from your mistakes. Then remind yourself of the relative insignificance of one bad workout or one bad race in the universal scheme of things.

After a series of bad workouts or races it's somewhat harder to remind yourself of that. A series of failures can drain away gumption until the well looks permanently dry. When in a slump, it's time to go over old ground, look for solutions, and go back to the things you know you can do well. Perhaps you make a change in your program. Sometimes any change may help. (Ever hear of the "Hawthorne Effect"? A famous study took place at the Western Electric Company's Hawthorne Plant in Chicago, Illinois. Researchers found that if they increased the illumination at a work area at the plant, the productivity increased. Interestingly, they found that when the illumination was turned *down*, productivity also increased, suggesting that *any* change may lead to improvement.[7])

Additionally, work to eliminate problems in your life outside of running—family, school, work, social life. Iron out things that are bugging you. Take care you're not overcommitting yourself emotionally.

Sometimes the best antidote may be to stop running altogether for a while. Take some mental health days. Head off the burned-out feeling. Let your subconscious work out your problems.

SIGNIFICANT OTHERS

"Keep away from people who try to belittle your ambitions. Small people always do that, but the really great make you feel that you, too, can become great."

Mark Twain

We are influenced by forces exerted by others, an infinite array of behaviors, of things people do and don't do, of strokes that sustain us and abrasions that sap our energy. A handshake, a nod, an encouraging word, a piece of true advice, a smile, a compliment, an approving look, a heart-to-heart talk, a cheer, a hug. A frown, a shove, a shun, a word behind your back, a disloyalty, a knock, an insensitive remark, a criticism, a boo, a lie.

The "loneliness of the long distance runner" aside, we are surrounded by others—parents, friends, lovers, teachers, co-workers, competitors, acquaintances. We move through a small sea of people, and there is an ebb and flow of energies, an interplay that profoundly influences our gumption for racing.

I've seen runners of extreme talent reduced to cinders and their racing destroyed by the people around them. I've also seen runners of little ability buoyed and inspired to great racing by the people around them.

Keeping before us Mark Twain's advice, let's look briefly at the "significant others" who surround runners to see how they can help or hinder.

Family and friends

One parent of a runner of mine regularly reduced his son to tears, criticizing him after poor races. I knew another father who would position himself at a strategic point in the race in order to swear at his son and yell, "You're doing it again! You're giving up!" Needless to say, the son didn't respond well to this type of encouragement.

There are spouses who are jealous of the other's time spent running, Little League parents for whom only the Olympic Gold will be enough, and friends who'd rather be anywhere else but at the track watching their friend run. These represent a category of gumption-sapper—people closest to us who, ironically, either knowingly or unknowingly, do their best to undermine our running.

Fortunately, the majority of families and friends are supportive. If asked, they will stand in the rain to offer encouragement, learning obscure names and the jargon of the times. They give counsel. Perhaps they join us. They celebrate with us when we succeed, console us when we fail, and remind us that our worth is measured in ways other than a 10K time.

Coaches

It was the morning of the Central Collegiate Championships in Chicago's Washington Park, and our team sat at breakfast talking

112

excitedly about a meet two weeks away. We had won the Big Eight Conference, thereby qualifying for the NCAA Championships in New York City. None of us had ever been to the Big Apple, and we were making plans. Coach didn't like the drift of our conversation. We should be thinking about today's meet. Casually he stated, "Oh, by the way, if you don't win the meet today, I'm not taking you to New York." We ate the rest of the meal in silence. We lost the Centrals by a point, a meet we should have won easily. The coach, despite his threat, took us to New York.

One runner is confused. The coach gave him much attention, praise, and good advice during his recruiting, but now, the busy coach appears twice a week to give the workouts. Another runner is irate. Coach has suggested, not subtly, that the injury is in the runner's head. Another runner is dispirited. He broke his personal best by twelve seconds in the mile. His coach's reaction—"Your mistake was not moving in the third quarter! Think!"

Sorry, coaches, but it's true. We do some awful things to our charges. We can be lethal to a runner's gumption.

We can also play an important role and offer tremendous help. The fact that most top runners, years after leaving school, still rely on the assistance of a coach suggests more than just habit. A coach, outside of guiding the athlete and imparting important technical knowledge about training and racing, also can provide a very useful perspective. Coaches can stand back, observe, and notice things, things the runner may not notice. Are the shoes worn down? Is the running form different? Why the pale complexion today? A good coach learns how the individual ticks. What, exactly, will *this* person's response be to *this* workout? How will he respond to *this* pressure situation? Can he train with *this* particular soreness? (When Peter Coe, Seb's father and coach, is asked for coaching tips, he admits that to be as successful with another as he has been with his son, he'd have to have that athlete living with him for years.)

A coach helps keep a rein on an athlete. Given their compulsive nature, runners always want to train hard one more day, race hard one more time too often. Coaches can help prevent injuries and sickness by keeping their charges from doing too much. Additionally, coaches save their runners a lot of work by making decisions about workouts, arranging the logistics of racing and training, lining up other resource people, and generally, by helping them see the forest through the trees. Good coaches help runners save much wasted emotional energy.

Of course, they can also help build emotional energy. Good ones muster up loads of positive reinforcement and wrap their athletes in it. (The importance of positive reinforcement is well documented. A study was done, for instance, with grade schoolers beginning a one-month fitness program. During the running practices, one group was given only criticism, one group was given only praise, and one control group was given a mixture of praise and criticism. As you might guess, the praised group, in races at the end of the program, beat the pants off everyone else.)

Great coaches are gumption generators, having a talent for inspiring others and making them believe in unlimited potential.

Running partners

Much of your practice time and running-related talk is with running partners. This being the case, partners represent another key energy field. Partners help make training more interesting and fun. Partners often are your biggest supporters; they know what you're capable of and can remind you.

But there are potential problems too. You run with a faster runner, and you find yourself two strides back, struggling and feeling emotional energy flow from you to him. You run with a slower runner and you brake to let him keep up, feeling slightly embarrassed and upset, and losing the quality of the workout. You run with a group and the competitive spirit pervades, turning your training sessions into all-out races, and leaving you burned out by the day of the meet.

So here again, a caveat becomes clear—Beware of gumption-sappers. Give thought to associating with true helpers. And in so far as considering the running ability of your partners, you would do well to follow the "one-third" rule. One-third of the time run with people who are a little better than you. One-third of the time train with those not as fast. One-third of the time, with your equals.

Opponents

Shotputter Parry O'Brien psyched out his opponents at the Melbourne Olympics, the story goes, by pointing at each of his rivals as they left the Olympic Village for the stadium, telling them:

"You'll get third . . . You'll get eighth . . . You'll get fifth."
Marty Liquori would run behind an opponent and play-act, letting
out a few groans of pain to delude the other into thinking Liquori
was about to break.

A special type of running "partner" is the person standing
next to you on the starting line. It doesn't take much thought to
realize you'd rather have your opponent there than not there. Competitors help you test your limits, drag out all the effort and ability
you have to give, bring out the best in you. Keep in mind the Latin
meaning of "compete": "to seek together."

Not that competition doesn't present problems. Competition
induces pressure. When you're running to beat the clock *plus* certain
other runners, you have more at stake. Also, competition distracts.
You may worry more about what your opponent is doing than what
you should be doing. (Think of the "cat and mouse game" Coe and
Ovett play when they race together.)

Also, with competition comes psychological warfare. From
imperious disregard, to the flashy uniform, to the solicitous concern, to the brag and the snide comment—almost everyone at some
time takes part in mind games. The racer's task is to be aware of the
various psychological ploys and be ready to deal with them, and
know how to put them to use if need be.

Your "pit crew"

Today's elite distance runner takes the philosophy of associating with helpful others to its logical end. He has a veritable pit crew
of helpers—podiatrists, managers, chiropractors, masseurs,
physiologists, psychologists, and shoe experts. As with the race car
driver, the pit crew has become a necessity for the elite runner. In a
sense, he's delegating to others some of the components of his
performing, and by relying on their expertise, he can circumvent
potential problems and save much time and emotional energy.

The ordinary jogger and Sunday road racer can employ some
of this same philosophy.

You may want to use specialists at some point. If you do, shop
around, for the ones who can best help you. When you find a doctor
who gets you through injuries quickly and consistently, and keeps
you running, stick with him! When you find a shoe salesman who
consistently puts you in shoes just right for you, stick with him!

115

ATTENTION TO DETAIL

The great baseball player Ty Cobb had an apparently nervous habit of kicking the bag whenever he was on first base. When he finally retired from the game, the reason for this behavior came out. Cobb could move the bag almost two inches closer to second base by kicking it. And this improved his chances for stealing second base or getting there safely on a ground ball.

In distance racing—as with the pursuit of excellence in any activity—the small things matter. Pay attention to detail. I once listened to a presentation by the great New Zealand coach, Arthur Lydiard. At one point during his talk, he spent several minutes explaining the proper technique for tying running shoes. He related stories of champions felled by blisters from loose shoes and by fractured metatarsals from tight shoes. Quality running, he emphasized, comes down to the fine points.

Here are several details demanding the runner's attention.

Staying healthy

Missing training days due to sickness or injury is the end of the world for most runners. Sitting home unable to train, only twenty-four hours after you were running happily down the roads, it seems like years since you were able to run—and years before you will feel good again. "Damn! I've got to start all over again!" Hiss . . . goes your gumption.

For runners, sickness and injury are occupational hazards. Hard training stresses the body. Each stride sends a shock through your body three times your weight. Muscle fiber is broken down and rebuilt. Your system struggles to adapt. Resistance to colds is lowered. Paradoxically, when your training is at its best, you're often at your most susceptible.

Most sickness and injury can be avoided by attending to details. Invariably, warning signs will tip you off: unusual fatigue, sleeplessness, loss of appetite, increased pulse rate, loose bowels, poor coordination, changed coloring, nervousness. If you're listening carefully to your body, you can cut back or stop your training *before* a breakdown.

The principles of staying healthy have been well publicized.

These principles include such things as adequate sleep, well-balanced diet, proper running shoes, sensible training, regular stretching, proper form, and prudent use of sports medicine. The problem is not that runners don't know these principles. They do. The problem comes in exercising the self-control to follow through on these principles consistently and meticulously.

Getting information

"To live effectively is to live with adequate information."

Norbert Wiener

The great mathematician's statement has particular relevance for runners. The better informed a runner is, the better he can race. Numerous runners have gotten burned because of lack of information—Miruts Yifter reporting to the wrong stadium gate and missing his Olympic final; Shorter knowing little about Cierpinski before the Montreal Marathon. Thorough planning and information-gathering help lessen pre-race anxiety and cut down the possibility of mistakes.

So read, study, keep notes. Understand the why's and wherefore's of your workouts. Keep notes on what you do, so you can refer back, compare, and revise for the future. Chart your progress. Log pulse rate, sleep, and diet so you get a daily picture of your physical machine. Know the race schedule, the course, and your competition. Has your opponent raced lately? How does he train? Is he a kicker or a pace runner? Find reliable sources. One top coach I know gets athletic journals from East Germany and has them translated into English. Now that's being informed!

GREAT EXPECTATIONS

Bill had a goal for the mile. One older brother of Bill's had run 4:31 in high school, and another brother had run a few seconds slower. With two months left in his senior year, Bill had a best of 4:33. He hoped to break 4:30 and set the "family record."

Bill had ability. He once ran 51.5 anchoring his team's mile relay. On another occasion, he bet he could run ten quarters under

66. Bill ran eleven averaging 63.2. Bill's coach seemed impatient with the 4:33 mile time. He urged Bill to go after the school record. Bill couldn't take the thought seriously. 4:16, set by some "animal" athlete twelve years ago—the record was out of sight! Besides, Bill figured, 4:33 was pretty good, good enough to win the conference anyway.

Bill eventually did go just under 4:30 winning the conference mile. But he never did see the writing on the wall. He went off to college and planned to go out for track, but when he learned the slowest runners on the team were running 4:20 he decided against it.

Steve also had a goal for the mile. His father had been a good miler, a high school state champion. The plaque was on the mantel at home: "First Place—4:30.5." Steve wanted to break 4:30. With two months left in his senior year, he had a best of 4:52.

When Steve was an eighth grader, everyone said, "Watch out! Here comes a great one!" No one his age could beat him. But Steve, an "early maturer," hadn't grown much since then. It was apparent to most that Steve would look more like his grandfather, built low to the ground and stocky. In high school several of Steve's teammates improved faster and had surpassed him.

Steve was bitter about his racing. "4:52 is terrible! I should be running much faster! I'm a wimp!" Every race he went out at 4:29 pace and then died. In his final meet of the season, Steve ran 4:47, a personal record, and never ran another step.

So far in this chapter we have discussed some of the external circumstances affecting the runner's energy. The rest of this chapter examines the internal runner, the thinking about races that runners commonly engage in. It proposes ways of thinking that are productive, that will fuel gumption and enhance racing.

One set of thoughts has to do with *expectations*. Your thoughts about how you will do in a race and how you ought to do have a profound impact on performance. They can set you up for success or set you up for failure. Reasonable expectations help you get the most out of yourself. They have a powerful, self-fulfilling effect. ("I set realistic goals for each mile," one marathoner recently told me. "I pictured each mile time. And, can you believe it, in the race, I hit every one!") Unreasonable goals, if they're too high, can lead to frustration and loss of gumption; if they're too low, they can limit, act as a brake to your progress—and cause loss of gumption.

The stories of Bill and Steve exemplify what can go wrong when your expectations get muddled. Bill expected too little from himself. Unwilling to let go of his 4:30 miler self-image, he closed his eyes to the signs showing him he was a much faster runner. Steve erred on the other end—his expectations were unrealistically high. He set just as arbitrary a goal as Bill's, neglected facts, and set himself up for frustration.

We are Bill and Steve. We lock ourselves into similar, arbitrary preconceptions. Rather than see ourselves for the runners we *are* (and see ourselves anew each day) and see each race situation for what it *is*, instead we put blinders on and see things as we *think they should be*. "Values rigidity" author Robert Pirsig calls this fault. "The inability to revalue what you see due to a commitment to previous values."[8] It's one of the biggest traps there is.

Getting hung up on preconceptions results in bad mental habits. The most prevalent form is the IMA, as in "I'm a kicker." The self-image of "I'm a kicker" may have originated from some past race or something someone once told you. And it may even serve you just fine. Until the day you get in a race with better kickers. If you adhere to your kicking strategy, you will lose. Or your IMA may serve you fine until the day you can't use your kick because you've relied on it exclusively and haven't developed stamina enough to handle a tough pace.

One of our country's latest marathon stars, Marianne Dickerson, exemplifies how we can get stuck with detrimental IMA's. A high school state champion at 800 meters, Dickerson went to college and competed in the middle distances. Despite the fact she showed great stamina, had efficient form, and could tolerate high mileage, her coaches saw her only as an 800–1500 runner. She experienced average success (having only above average leg speed) until the end of her senior year when she demanded to run 10,000 meters. In her second 10,000 meter race, the AIAW Championships, she placed third. One year later, when she moved up to the marathon, she discovered even more ability. In only her third marathon, she placed second in the 1983 Helsinki World Championships. How fortunate it was that she saw her way clear of the IMA "middle distance runner"!

Here are several other IMA's which commonly afflict runners:

"I'm a front runner."
"I'm a *(insert a time)* miler."
"I'm a poor runner in the rain."
"I'm not a winner."
"I'm injury-prone."
"I'm no good in big meets."

IMA's prevent us from seeing things as they are, and invariably, the result is limitation or frustration or both. With clear thinking and diligence, you can rid yourself of undermining IMA's.

Understand why IMA's exist and work to eliminate them

Knowing the reasons why you fall prey to IMA's may help you steer clear of them. We use "scripts" for convenience sake (some would say laziness). IMA's allow us to manage our world more easily. It's hard looking at everything anew and without preconceptions, so we put things in pigeonholes, including ourselves. IMA's also allow us to avoid unpleasant tasks. By saying "I'm not a big meet racer," you can conveniently avoid pressure situations. Lack of sufficient information is another reason for IMA's. If you've never raced 10,000 meters, it may be hard for you to see beyond "I'm a middle-distance runner."

Catch yourself when you use an IMA. Break old scripts. Tell yourself, "I chose to be this way *until today*." Tackle the thing you've been avoiding. Make your goal simply to tackle it.

See your running as it is

Study your best time for your event, shrewdly assess what is possible, and set your next goal accordingly. Control your ego, look at the runner you are. Give yourself and each race situation a fresh look because you and the circumstances of each race change. Perhaps you used to follow and draft off others, but now you've progressed to where you should lead races and go for time. It's a fallacy to think your history of racing should determine your present racing. Be open-minded enough to see new developments.

Set realistic goals

Look at the expected "improvement curve" for runners. It's reasonable to expect an improvement of one to ten seconds per year per mile. Have short-range, intermediate, and long-range goals. Base them on what you've already accomplished. Make them attainable and progressive. If you're an inexperienced runner, get someone to help you set goals. But make sure the goals are *yours*.

Get all the facts

Base your expectations on facts, not fantasies. To get a real picture of what you can do in races, look at the telling facts before you. Look at your workouts. If your best set of quarters is twelve at seventy seconds, what kind of mile should you run? If you're aiming for 5:00 next race, you're not expecting enough from yourself. Know what your workouts augur. Look at your past races. If your best mile is 5:01, and you're shooting for a sub-4:30 next race, you're deluding yourself. Look at physiological facts. Check your pulse rate—monitor the changes. Track your weight and percentage of body fat. If you have access to the machines, test your maximum oxygen uptake and your anaerobic threshold. Have your blood composition analyzed (these are regular procedures in East German sports institutes). Get the facts. Look also at what other runners who are similar to you have done. And look at the talent you have . . . but be careful.

"Natural talent" is a dangerous phrase invented probably by those who want to pigeonhole others and sap gumption. The phrase is used a lot with athletes—"He's got great natural talent," or "He lacks natural talent." The phrase is used almost reverently, and it makes for a convenient final answer to most questions about an athlete's performance.

When people say a runner has "natural talent," they usually mean that person has been born with certain physical characteristics that are 1) relevant and helpful to distance racing, and 2) the kind that can't (at least to any great extent) be put into a runner later by training or other "outside" means. What are the physical characteristics which fulfill these two conditions?

Leg speed, most argue, is one. Physiologists have found mus-

121

cle fiber is not all the same, that there are "fast twitch" fibers and "slow twitch" fibers. Runners with a higher percentage of "fast twitch" muscle are better able to contract the muscle faster, and hence, have faster turnover, or sprint-speed. The composition of your muscle fiber can't be changed. So you're stuck with the sprint speed you have, right?

Not quite. How fast your leg muscles contract is just one piece to the leg speed picture. Another piece is how powerfully you can contract the muscle, or leg strength. Leg strength can be improved by training. Another piece is your fluidity, your running form. Form can be improved through practice. In reality, leg speed can be considerably improved. Consider Valery Borzov, 1972 Olympic Champion for 100 and 200 meters. At fourteen, Borzov ran 13.0 for 100 meters, an average time for that age. In eight years Borzov cut off *three full seconds*, the result of masterful training and scientific scrutiny.[9]

Tests have shown that good sprinters have anywhere from 65 percent to 85 percent fast-twitch muscle fiber and middle distance runners have 70 percent to 35 percent fast twitch. Keep in mind, therefore, one additional point: The actual percentage of fast-twitch muscle you have may be plenty fast enough because there is a *broad range* wherein sprinting excellence lies.

Natural talent proponents cite maximum oxygen consumption as another fixed trait. How good your system is at taking in oxygen and getting it to your muscles is a crucial factor in racing success, and studies have shown that after only two months of training, your maximum oxygen uptake—VO_2 max—doesn't change much. But here too, as with leg speed, there is more to the picture.

Your VO_2 max is akin to an automobile's official miles per gallon rating—it suggests the upper limits of performance. If you put ten cars on the line, all with an MPG rating of 40, and give each of them one gallon of gasoline, would the cars all run out of gas and stop at the same point forty miles out from the line? A car's use of the gasoline would depend on numerous factors: how well-tuned the car was, how well-oiled, how skilled the driver. If you put ten runners on the line, all with a VO_2 max of 70 (ml./kg./min.), would they finish in a dead heat? Numerous factors enter into how the runners use their oxygen. The ability to get by on a smaller percentage of VO_2 max, the ability to cope with a higher oxygen debt, the use of efficient form, the ability to relax—these factors would separate the runners. And these factors can each be improved considerably by practice.

Also, top distance runners have been tested and have shown a VO_2 max anywhere from 64 (ml./kg./min.) to 84. Frank Shorter (71.4) and Steve Prefontaine (84.4) ran the same three-mile time, and yet there was a considerable difference in their VO_2 max (13 ml/kg.min.).[10] Therefore, just as with percentage of fast-twitch muscle fiber, there is a broad range of VO_2 max which may enable you to run with the best of them.

Consider too, other "relevant" characteristics that are truly unalterable, like your age or your size. Certainly these characteristics will place some limitations on you. Yet, think of Olympians Gerry Lindgren at 17 and Jack Foster at 42. And size? Jack Bachelor at 6'7" and Miruts Yifter at 5'4" were both pretty fair distance runners. Remember when the large, muscular Alberto Juantorena was the "runner of the future"? Then along came Sebastian Coe.

Don't get hung up on "talent." The things people point to when they talk about your "talent" or your "potential," when scrutinized, turn out to be either not so unalterable or not so singularly crucial to quality distance racing. "Studies of distance runners indicate there is no single predictor of success," says Dr. David Costill. " 'Talent' is a composite of many factors."[11] The factors represent broad ranges of possibilities and probabilities within which your performance might fall. If you have 90 percent slow-twitch muscle fiber, the probability of your becoming a world class sprinter is low. If you have VO_2 max of 40, the chances of your hanging with Alberto Salazar in the last mile of a 10K are slim.

When you think about how well you can run, you should consider things like your VO_2 max. But be careful to get all the facts and look at the whole picture.

Dream dreams

If you're smart about your goals, if you learn the art of moving them out further and further but each time barely within your grasp, if you pursue them with hard work, enthusiasm, dedication, and patience, and if you keep open-minded about your chances, then great achievements are possible.

An open-minded athlete once challenged the "ultimate barrier" of human endurance, the four-minute mile. His sub-four race was seen as a miracle performance. Hundreds since then have gone under this "barrier." Now a 3:59 mile in a world class race would put you a straightaway behind the winner.

Glenn Cunningham, whose legs were burned so badly as a child that doctors told him he'd never walk, went on to set the world record in the mile. More than most sports, distance racing shows that the only limits to performance are the limits you place on yourself.

DIRE CONSEQUENCES

Your thoughts about how you will do in a race are closely intertwined with thoughts about the *consequences* of your race performance. Rarely are you without a few of the "what if's." "What if I can't handle the pace?" "What if I psych out?" "What if I have a lousy race and waste all the hard work I've done?" "What if I fail in front of all my friends?" These thoughts of dire consequences can wage guerrilla warfare against the strongest psyche, increase anxiety, and drag down your gumption.

Fears about failing arise. You've set a reasonable goal for your race, now the thought—"What if I don't hit my goal, then what?" Then it's self-contempt time. "I'll let myself down. I'll wimp out. I'm basically a lower form of life, and somehow, for my next race, I'll have to pick myself out of the gutter." And self-pity. "I put in *all* this work. I made *all* these sacrifices. All for nothing."

I should say parenthetically it's very hard not to think thoughts like this and not to feel pressure when considering the object of your keen desire. Pressure seems to rise in direct relation to the size of your emotional investment, the size of the stakes. Ironically, increased pressure only gets more in the way between you and your goal. A Chinese wise man once observed: "When an archer is shooting for enjoyment, he has all his skills; when he shoots for a brass buckle he gets nervous, when he shoots for a prize of gold, he begins to see two targets."

Your fears of failing also have to do with thoughts of embarrassing yourself in front of others. From the first, parents, teachers, and peers cause some pressure as we try to meet up to their expectations. Fail—and we are subject to their disapproval.

I coached a runner once who raced beautifully almost every race. The exceptions were the days his father would show up to watch him; on those days the boy would fall apart.

Fear of failure creates many fascinating avoidance behaviors. There are at least a hundred ways to let yourself off the hook for a race. I think I've seen them all and used many myself.

There are things you do and think beforehand that provide a convenient excuse for not running well.

"I ran hard all week . . . I'm running through this meet."
"I was out late last night."
"I got to the race late. I missed my warm-up."

There are the faint-of-heart decisions made at race-time.

"I'll run this race as a workout."
"I just can't get psyched up for this race."
"I just need to feel good in this race. I'll save the full effort for next race."

There are the creative excuses made after the race.

"I had a terrible start."
"My shoes felt loose the whole way."
"I hated the course."
"I looked up and the leaders were gone!"

I've also seen the more perverse varieties of avoidance. Some runners always seem to get sick or injured at the most inopportune times. "Damn, I was really ready, but I got sick again." Some simply enjoy doing penance. "I'm sorry. I don't know what happened. I'm really sorry."

All these cop-outs beg the question—Why didn't you go all out as you should have? The honest answer would be—The thought of running all out and failing is too troubling.

Beleaguering thoughts about what dire consequences the race may bring include more than just fears of failure. *Fears about winning* can be just as troubling. Winning raises the stakes. With winning come bigger and bigger races and crowds, better competition, more intense publicity, bigger prizes, and more severe expectations to defend your titles and race up to your billing. It's no wonder some runners actually fear winning. I've had runners capable in every way of being champions but who, whenever they got too close, would take one step back, and keep winning and the responsibilities it would bring at arm's length.

We must empathize with the race "favorite" and the pressures he brings on himself. I once had a runner who went into our unofficial indoor state meet as one of a dozen good milers in the state. He ran beautifully, emerged the victor, and immediately became "the favorite" to win the outdoor state meet. Now the monkey was on his back, and it stayed there all spring. In his thinking, since everyone now expected him to win, anything less would be a blow-up, a disgrace. The rest of the season he never ran with the same verve and spontaneity—and ended up losing in the state meet.

The difficult position of the favorite and the advantage of the underdog are well known. The favorite can assume certain attitudes to lessen his pressure, which we'll get into next, yet the situations of the favorite and the underdog raise one interesting consideration. Is it always in a runner's best interest to win? Would it be more helpful to go into a later, more important race, without the pressure of being the favorite? In the 1983 Rotterdam Marathon, Salazar lost to de Castella. It was a "major loss" for Salazar, but perhaps was not so bad, taking the monkey off his back and putting it on de Castella's for the year leading up to the Olympics.

It's easy to get hung up about winning and losing because our thinking is so ingrained in our culture's ideas about things. Many of our cultural ideas, when examined closely, turn out to be patently ridiculous and irrational.

Psychiatrist Albert Ellis and other modern thinkers have done much to point up the fallacies in certain societal notions. Ellis' "rational-emotive therapy" tests the preconceived notions causing us so much anxiety. Sports psychologists use Ellis' rational-emotive therapy in counseling athletes. His ideas can be applied easily and beneficially to distance racing.[12]

Fallacy No. One: You must succeed in every race to consider yourself worthwhile.

First, succeeding in every race is impossible. Human beings just don't work that way. You are going to have bad races occasionally. The compulsion that you *have to* race well every time only leads to anxiety. The main fallacy here comes when you define your self-worth by how well you race. You are not your races. Running a bad race doesn't mean you are bad.

The healthiest course is to accept your failures and understand they are necessary. They force you to analyze the mistakes you made in the race, and that's how you learn. Also, rather than getting preoccupied with the *outcome* of your race, enjoy the *process* of racing, the trying, the challenge, the risk taking. Put your emotional energy there rather than in the outcome.

Fallacy No. Two: You must succeed in every race to insure the approval of others.

Outside of the fact that this goal is again, impossible, the idea that if you race poorly, all your significant others will suddenly dissapprove of you is clearly ridiculous. It won't happen, and if you do have friends turn away from you, it's *their* hang-up, not yours.

Be careful too about *needing* the approval of others. You end up using their measures of success, thinking, for example, that anything after first place in a race is lousy. (In this school of thought, Ron Clarke, Jim Ryun, Marty Liquori, and Derek Clayton were lesser runners because they never won an Olympic Gold Medal.) Define your own standards of success. Gain self-approval first. Rather than getting preoccupied with others' approval, direct your energy on the task at hand, the race.

Fallacy No. Three: It is a horrible thing when races don't turn out the way you want them to.

Is having a bad race really so horrible? Here's one pre-race question I've always found helpful: "What is the *worst* thing that could happen to me if I fail in this race?" The answer never seems very awful. Accept the fact you are going to fail in races occasionally, that it's far from the worst thing in the world, that no single race is that important and getting upset certainly won't help the matter. Instead, *use* your failures to good advantage. Learn from them, work on solutions. Use them to inspire you to greater efforts.

127

Fallacy No. Four: Races will generate pressure over which you have no control.

First, remember it is not the *race* that causes your anxiety—it is *your thinking* about the race. And as this book has shown, you can control your thinking. By mental rehearsal, positive self-affirmation, and other techniques it's possible to change and control the content of your thoughts to enhance performance.

Make up your mind to tackle the things you fear and desensitize yourself to them. Also, don't be surprised if some nervousness in race situations remains. That is natural—even the coolest Olympic champions feel it.

Fallacy No. Five: It's easier to avoid difficult races than face up to them.

By not laying it on the line and going flat out in a race, initially you save yourself the discomfort of a hard race. But in the long run, it is much more uncomfortable to avoid hard racing. Self-incrimination is inevitable, and your resulting nonsuccess breeds frustration and dissatisfaction. Eventually your avoidance may become habitual.

Gumption comes from *doing*, not avoiding. *Doing* is where the real fun of racing lies. Be wary of things that get you off the hook—a slight ache in your foot, the chance for a late night before the race, a racing partner ("Let's run this as a workout."), an "innocent" IMA ("I'm not the kind of runner who can take out the pace hard."). Shun the avenues to avoidance. Find ways to lock yourself into laying it on the line in a race. Make a bet with someone. Get on a relay and be responsible to your three teammates. Tell your rival that you're out to beat him.

THE RIGHT STUFF

"Some could ask, 'Well, if I get around all those gumption traps, then will I have the thing licked?'

"The answer, of course, is no, you still haven't got anything licked. You've got to live right too. It's the way you live that predisposes you to avoid the traps and see the right facts. You want to know how to paint a perfect painting? It's easy. Make yourself perfect and then just paint naturally. That's the way all the experts do it. The making of a painting or the fixing of a motorcycle isn't separate from the rest of your existence . . ."[13]

Robert Pirsig

To paraphrase Pirsig—If you want to run perfect races, make yourself perfect, and then just run naturally.

Mustering your emotional energy and channeling it into your running paves the way to perfect races. But you don't necessarily end up there if you don't "live right, too." You might have all the race-gumption in the world, but lack the self-control to store it and use it in the last quarter of the race. You might be able to skirt every energy trap, but lack the desire and patience to wait ten years for your best racing.

I don't pretend to know all the "right stuff" that makes a perfect racer, though I know some of the attributes, and I wouldn't presume to tell you how to get them, though I feel the attributes can be developed, just as gumption can be built, and that they're not fixed commodities.

I'd like to suggest a few of these attributes and pose some related questions and ideas about the perfect racer.

Diligence

How hard are you willing to work to improve your running? The sport, ultimately, takes a lot of hard work. As the body adapts to work loads, it requires increasing work loads if it is to keep getting stronger. There is no getting around the fact that becoming faster and stronger takes pounding on the roads and sprinting on the tracks, and it'll require an increasingly greater intensity.

Desire

How fierce is your desire to achieve in running? How badly do you want to hit your time, win the race, or beat your rival? How

129

much will it bother you if you don't? How much of yourself will you give to the pursuit? How much will you sacrifice?

Your desire is tested in training when you look out at the pouring rain and decide whether to run. And your desire will be tested in the last lap when your legs are seething with lactic acid, your rival is at your shoulder, and you're ready to make an internal bargain you will later regret.

How hungry are you?

Discipline

If desire is the *wanting*, then discipline is *remembering what you want*. Do you have the strength of mind to adhere to a routine? Do you have the will not to miss days? I've known runners who've gone years without missing a day of running. Whether it's in an airport or in a hotel stairway, they always seem to find a time and place to run.

Discipline also means having the self-control not to run when you shouldn't and not sprint in a race when you shouldn't.

Self-Belief

An invaluable attribute to bring to the starting line is a strong belief in yourself and the fact you've done everything right to get ready for the race. Doubt drains gumption, whereas belief generates it.

Do you change your program constantly? Find out what works best for you and stick to it. Develop a program that is special to your needs, that you understand, that incorporates your likes and the things that make you confident, one that gets results. When it comes right down to it, the actual specifics of your training are not nearly as important as your belief in them. There have been great milers who have thrived on thirty miles per week and others who have thrived on one hundred and thirty. If you *believe* that sprinting once around the block every night at midnight is the right training for you, then it will be.

Interest

Repetitiveness being the nature of distance running, there lurks an omnipresent foe—boredom. Boredom can turn your races into training runs and your training runs into drudgery.

How well can you maintain your interest in things? Only by keeping a fascination with your running can you bring to it spontaneity and clear-sightedness. A thing or an activity cannot be boring, Zen teaches; only *people get bored*. There are no boring runs, only bored (and boring) runners. Conquer the tendency to get bored. Be a student of the sport. See variety in each day.

Patience

Closely related to boredom is impatience. Never underestimate the amount of time it takes to get to quality racing. The impatient don't make it in running. People seeking immediate gratification need not apply. What running holds in store is *waiting*—waiting until the proper mileage base is accomplished (One European coach tells younger runners, "Run distance for ten years, then come back and see me.")—waiting out injuries. (Toshihiko Seko recently reflected on how his 18-month layoff due to injuries was good for developing patience.) And waiting in races. The best marathoners learn to wait, conserve energy, let their opponents run themselves out, and then strike.

Perspective

Given the compulsive nature of runners, many find it difficult to keep their running in perspective. "Perspective" means things such as:

- not jumping off a bridge after a bad race;
- not running when injured;
- being able to befriend your opponents;
- not seeing every race as an Olympic final and not seeing an Olympic final as the Judgment Day;
- enjoying the present;

- seeing the giant oak within the acorn;
- not getting preoccupied with past or future glories;
- talking about other things at parties besides running;
- not proselytizing around nonrunners;
- being able to win and lose gracefully;
- being able to savor your victories;
- knowing there are things more important than running;
- remembering sports are for fun;
- not spending a lot of money on the sport;
- seeing the good aspects of your bad races and the bad aspects of your good races;
- running your races and not others';
- helping others through a race;
- missing a day of running without cutting your throat;
- letting your races talk for you;
- taking risks, experimenting;
- seeing past one week or one season to a career of running.

"Give it your all!" The well-wisher's exhortation before our races is easily and automatically given and received. And yet the phrase can make us distance runners pause and think. Because for our sport, "give it your all" is especially relevant advice. Races have a way of greedily taking all we can give. Races, at the same time, never cheat: we get out of them every bit as much as we put in. And this give and take—what a felicitious exchange it is! When we are charged with vitality, we are racing well, and when we are racing well, we are charged with vitality.

So yes, indeed, give it your all!

CHAPTER SIX

What the Experts Say

What can we learn from the elite runners on the topic of psychological preparation? It's fair to assume, I think, because these runners consistently perform well in pressure situations, they know a few things about their "inner game." How do Alberto Salazar, Mary Decker, and other top runners get themselves psychologically ready for a race? How do they cope with the pressure? What do they think about in races? How do they deal with pain? To find out what they had to say on these topics, I sent out questionnaires to many of our nation's top distance runners. I asked them to respond to these questions and to explain their mental approach to racing.

Their responses were candid and thoughtful. Though few mentioned any formal psychological training, their answers often suggested a methodical planning, as well as a personalized approach. Here is what they had to say.

QUESTION 1.

What do you do prior to a race to get psychologically ready?

DICK BEARDSLEY (2:08.53 Boston Marathon '82, second fastest American time)

Depending on how important the race is, I usually start mentally preparing myself 3–6 weeks before the event. I try to visualize how the race will go. And how I could make the most of it. I also like to find out whom I'll be running against. I also feel much more confident if I can see the course before the race.

DOUG BROWN (three-time Olympian in steeplechase)

I picture the race in my mind several or more times—usually with me winning it. Sometimes I picture it with different types of strategies, and generally I'll end up with one appropriate plan as the race approaches.

MARY DECKER (World record holder in 10,000 meters, American record holder in mile, 1,500 meters, and 3,000 meters)

I don't really do anything special. I think my psychological preparation is a natural process that comes from being competitive.

MARIANNE DICKERSON (Silver Medalist World Championships Marathon)

My mental preparation for a big race begins weeks before the actual event. I often find myself mentally picturing myself in the racing situation during workouts. I'll picture myself surging past competitors or crossing the finish line in a certain time. I always try to visualize positive race results!

I honestly believe psychological preparation is as important as physical preparation! You can be the strongest, fittest athlete, but if you don't believe you can win, you won't.

KERRY DICKSON (two-time All-American in cross-country)

In high school, I used to think about how I planned to run a race and what I expected other runners to do. I also used to tell myself I was ready for the race.

Now in college, I use a more refined and elaborate method of achieving the same objectives. It is a form of mental training using deep muscle relaxation and mental imagery.

MIKE DURKIN (two-time Olympian in 1,500 meters)

A race was always the culmination of the physical preparation that preceded it. I always attempted to comprehend my level of ability and shape for each race; this varied throughout the course of the season. If a race occurred during that portion of the season when I was still getting into shape, training hard and not backing off, I would honestly appraise that and attempt to run hard to that level or a bit higher—being more concerned with pushing myself for improvement rather than running strategically. Doing that allowed me to push the pace or move out farther from the finish by driving hard, without fearing a failure, without fearing losing or dying in the stretch. If that happened, so be it—so long as I carried the race a bit farther than the last time. My shape dictated this. I didn't put pressure on myself, except to run to my "apparent" limit at that point.

Later, when I felt in racing shape (as opposed to training shape), I would look for positive physical feedback: doing more work with less strain, flowing in workouts, feeling fresher, sharper. These signals got me "up." Racing then tended to be a natural extension or reward for all the work that preceded it. When I was racing at that time of the season, psychology was an afterthought. I *knew* as the season progressed that I was stronger—and that physical progress was my mental preparation.

JOHN GREGOREK (1980 and 1984 Olympian in steeplechase)

Usually the entire week before a race I like to concentrate on what I'm going to do and establish some sort of plan. There are certain races that I'll plan my entire season around and I'll concentrate on these weeks, even months, before. Right before a race I'll try to listen to some music and forget about everything except the race. Warming up and stretching sufficiently help me gain additional confidence.

JIM HILL (NCAA All-American in 5,000 meters)

By structuring workouts to different racing situations, I am able to simulate the race experience mentally and physically. Preparation also occurs right up until the start of the race. By reviewing my opponents' strengths and weaknesses and comparing them to my own, I am able to mentally picture the multitude of racing situations. Also, by realizing that on a given day an unknown factor may determine the outcome, I try to prepare myself accordingly.

STEVE LACY (1980 Olympian in 1,500 meters, 1984 Olympian in 5,000 meters)

I prepare a race plan which will accommodate as many of the potential race variations as possible. After a race plan is formulated, I try not to dwell upon the competition at all. I try to keep myself busy until it's time to warm up. During the warm-up, I replay my race plans(s).

135

JOHN LODWICK (2.10 marathoner)

I think of the race, the distance, and the pace. I pray that God will be honored by the way I compete and that I'll do the best I can and leave the results to Him.

DOUG PADILLA (1983 TAC Champion, 1984 Olympian in 5,000 meters)

I consider the competition and determine the type of race that I'll need to run in order to win. I make a decision before the race as to where I'll make my move and then determine that I won't allow myself to be broken until I make my move. Then I pray that I'll be mentally tough to keep contact. I also remind myself that the race is going to hurt and that I should expect pain.

BILL RODGERS ('76 Olympian, four-time winner of the New York and Boston Marathons).

I go over the course thoroughly. I stay as calm and rested as possible in the days prior to a race. I plan the pre-race preparations (travel, etc.) thoroughly. I avoid hectic situations—too much press, clinic work, etc.—as much as possible. I go over my good, solid preparation for the race. I go over my solid credentials vs. the competition's. I never automatically assume someone is "fitter" or a "better runner," etc. I make them "honest" as competitors.

ALBERTO SALAZAR (World record holder in marathon, American record holder in 5,000 meters and 10,000 meters)

I try to think about what my goals are for that particular race and what I'll have to do in order to reach those goals. I try to imagine what it's going to feel like and what I may encounter during the race from the competitors, the course, etc.

JIM SPIVEY (NCAA Champion and 1984 Olympian in 1,500 meters, Sports Festival 5,000 meters Champion)

My stretching routine during workouts is always the same. That way, before a race, I have a pattern set. Two hours before a race, I run through the pattern. Then one hour before, I run for thirteen to fourteen minutes and go through the pattern again. While I am stretching, I will try to run the race over in my

136

mind, trying to determine all the possible situations that could arise. If there's a [Steve] Scott in the race, I try to build up the image of myself, looking back to prior races and workouts. Post-race evaluation is an important factor. I will always determine what I did right or wrong and try to apply these lessons to future races. Some day you would hope you have learned all the lessons!

JIM STINTZI (NCAA All-American in 5,000 meters)

I take note of who my opponents are and how the race is likely to be run; i.e., whether it is to my advantage to lead or to follow, etc.

I constantly remind myself that the race will be harder (physically) than I expect, so that when the most difficult part of the race comes along, I am not taken by surprise.

CRAIG VIRGIN (Three-time Olympian in 10,000 meters, two-time International Cross-Country Champion)

My pre-race psychological preparation comes about usually from getting into the race site the day before the competition. I like to go over the proposed race site in practice the day before. I envision how the race will unfold, and I try to picture what my competition will do.

I study and analyze the terrain (if it is a cross-country or road-race course) and look for areas in a course in which to make my move so as to catch my opponents at their psychological and physiological weak points.

Other than that, I like to live as normal a life as possible. I like to have a nice, relaxed evening dinner before the race.

I try to get as close to eight hours of sleep as possible. If I have three to five hours before the race in the morning, I'll have my normal pre-race breakfast, which consists of a small stack of pancakes, a couple of fried eggs, a couple of cups of coffee with cream and sugar, and a glass of water.

QUESTION 2

What do you do to deal with the nervousness and pressure that may come with a big race?

BEARDSLEY:

The last few days before the race, I like to be by myself or only with real close friends. I also will go for walks by *myself* in the evening and think about what is coming up. I feel this is very important to me and it helps me relax before a big race.

BROWN:

I talk to other runners or competitors about the race. Usually you'll find they're as nervous as you are, and it helps you relax.

DECKER:

I concentrate on relaxing. I do other things to keep my mind occupied so as not to dwell on being nervous.

DICKERSON:

I try to deal with pre-race nervousness by spending time with someone who relaxes me and can take my mind off the race. My sister is a real comedian, she has a way of making me relax, laugh, and feel good before a race.

I think anyone, be it the weekend jogger or "world class" runner, is bound to experience nervousness before a competition. I try to build confidence by recalling all the hard training sessions I've put in.

DICKSON:

In high school I got sick and threw up before many races.

Now, I feel little difference in race pressures. I want to run the best race I can, so I concentrate on my individual feelings and preparations rather than the race pressures.

DURKIN:

I think I tried to prepare for each race the same way—maybe I was a bit more relaxed for "smaller" races, but I always attempted to approach each race in the same fashion. The mental preparation for a race, the time when the race was what you were focusing on (not the times you would find your thoughts casually turning to it), by and large, was put off until I was warming up for the race. That's not to say I didn't think of strategy, etc. in the days preceding the race. But I really focused on the race itself when I was warming up. And this I tended to do by following a set routine of physical activities—and as I moved from one preparation to another, I knew I was shutting out other thoughts and readying my body and mind for those brief moments of intense stress and activity. I wouldn't "psych" myself up—it was more a case of shutting out extraneous thoughts and moving from warming up, to stretching, to build-ups, to putting on my singlet, to finally putting on my spikes, to peeling off my sweats, and then, once reaching the line, *concentrating* on relaxing, staying calm and alert, being conscious of my form, keeping good position. All these were like steps up a ladder, and I tried to follow the same approach for an all-comers meet or the Olympic Games. I relaxed until I had to go off and start my warm-up routine. It got to be like a superstition, but having that routine allowed me to concentrate and get positive feedback and reinforcement from the familiarity of it.

GREGOREK:

I tell myself that what I'm feeling is actually what I enjoy about racing. The bigger the race, the more fun running is, and the nervousness comes along with it. My coach, Joe Long, will tell me that if I feel a lot of pressure or am unsure about anything, to let him make the decisions on what to do and how to race, and therefore the pressure is slightly removed from me. I really do enjoy a little pressure and try to think of it as something positive.

HILL:

Nervousness generated by any race situation has always, in the past, benefited me. Though I don't understand the physiology of the nervously aroused body, I feel that if an individual believes it will benefit him, then it most likely will.

I would like to believe that any pressure created by a race is in direct proportion to my own goals. With this in mind, I can deal with the race while dismissing the pressure.

LACY:

I try to have confidence in my training program and race plan, try to have confidence in my experience, try to identify why this

139

competition is important to *me*, and try to de-emphasize pressures that have no importance to *my* goals (i.e., press).

LODWICK:

I view nervousness as an aid. I don't get too nervous before a race. I try to see the race as God sees it—an event that has no eternal significance, save what is done for His honor and glory. I try to seize the moment, try to really enjoy the event and be thankful I can be a part of it. I pray that God will be honored in the race and that it will all be in His hands. I pray that I may do the best I can and that the results will be in His hands.

PADILLA:

I try to keep calm and not worry about getting real ready. If the race is big, then I worry more about getting too up than I do about mental preparation. As always, prayer is a big part. Not that I'll win, but that I'll run a smart race and not give up due to pain and the pressure during the race.

RODGERS:

Experience is a major factor in controlling fears. I use the adrenaline by controlling it during the race and understanding that prior to the race, it's a natural sign of pre-competition preparation by your mind/body. I also don't fidget, or move around a lot, or waste energy. I just rest.

SALAZAR:

I try to go over my workouts and races to see what condition I'm in to assure myself that I'm ready. I realize that nervousness is common and it's nothing to be ashamed or scared of.

SPIVEY:

I know that if I build myself up to a point to run with anyone, and then the race is a lot easier than I had expected, I become depressed after winning. The USA/USSR dual meet is an example. The two Russians had run 3:35 (1500 meters), and I expected the race to be the greatest of my life, but it turned out to be like another conference meet.

STINTZI:

First of all, I enjoy it. The pressure, the nervousness are all part of what makes racing (as opposed to just running) fun. I enjoy seeing how well I can race under all sorts of circumstances. I see each race as a challenge. Each race has different opponents and different strategies. It's a challenge to see what I can do in a given situation.

I pray (literally) that I won't be overcome by needless worrying. Worrying simply wastes my time and accomplishes nothing in terms of the outcome of the race itself.

VIRGIN:

In regards to nervousness and pressure that come before a big race, I feel that this is what separates the men from the boys. Through experience I have developed confidence that I can always perform up to my potential in any given racing situation. I just don't think about having a bad race. I concentrate on what the job is I have at hand. I study who my competition is and try to determine what kind of form they are presently exhibiting. I think about how my training has gone and I try to picture in my mind, using imagery, etc., how the race will be won and what it will feel like to win.

I think everyone gets nervous before a race, and I try to confine it to the last forty-five minutes or so before the gun goes off. I try to use that nervousness to develop as much adrenaline as possible.

QUESTION 3:

During a race, what do you think about?

BEARDSLEY:

Basically, I monitor the other runners and try to get an idea of how they're feeling. Basically, I am really concentrating on the race, trying to run as smoothly as possible, and thinking about getting to the finish line first before anyone else.

BROWN:

I'm constantly evaluating my pace and how I feel. I try to establish a comfortable rhythm that's going to max me out but not

141

force me into oxygen debt. It's a fine line . . . [This skill] improves with age and experience, and I believe most good runners are born with an innate talent for this. I also think about and evaluate the competition—how do they look—better yet, how do they sound. I try to pick up any indicators they may be sending out.

DECKER:

Relaxing, finishing, winning, and running fast. Also I am conscious of lap splits and not breaking form.

DICKERSON:

I try to relax and think about my goal for the race. I think about finishing and how good I'll feel if I attain that goal.

Again, I try to think of positive things. Toward the end of a marathon, for example, instead of thinking "I've got three miles to go!" I'll think of my favorite three-mile loop at home that I often jog comfortably with my Mom.

DICKSON:

During a good race, I think about many things, but nothing specifically. Things such as splits, other runners, internal feelings, people in the crowd, coach's instructions all are registered and responded to, but not concentrated on.

DURKIN:

The dominant thought I have in races is to constantly keep checking myself to run with good, efficient form and to run the race at the most relaxed effort possible. Races for me were in two stages—preliminary and the finish. All attention in the preliminary phase is to stay out of trouble (boxes, etc.) and just flow along—mentally "drafting" on the other racers . . . to get into the pace and try to keep it effortless.

The finish was very much the same as the first—run as hard as possible, but keep it smooth, not frantic. Power can flow from you, or you can press and cut off that flow. The biggest "head game" I would play in a race was deciding where to make my move and then mentally "gathering myself," mentally holding myself back until I reached that point—and then moving decisively. Also knowing at what point you can go to that last gear, but pretending you still have one more if necessary.

GREGOREK:

It depends on the race. For a small race, I try to remind myself that I'm in the race mainly for training and I'll tell myself just to run along as if I were on a hard training run.

For a big race, I recall all that I had been thinking and planning for the race. I try to think of relaxing all the parts of my body and my breathing.

HILL:

A single answer to this question is not available. I have thought everything from perfecting a planned strategy to daydreaming about any subject which might happen to pop in my mind.

LACY:

In a race that I perform well in, I do one of two things. Either I don't think about anything (completely blank), and I react to the things around me. Or I concentrate completely on the race . . . the positions of competitors, splits, etc.

In a race in which I do poorly, my mind tends to wander, or dwell on pain or on worries about failing.

LODWICK:

The race, pace, position, distance covered and distance to be covered. I concentrate on running as fast and as effectively as I can . . . and on specific Bible passages that may relate to competition, such as I Corinthians 10:31, Isaiah 45:24, Colossians 3:23-24.

PADILLA:

I concentrate on the runners ahead of me and think about keeping contact. I'm waiting for the time to make my move and hoping that it will come quick. I'm also concerned about getting boxed and not being able to react to a surge or move by someone else. I also try to make my speed changes gradual if reacting to someone else. That's more efficient. But if I'm trying to get away from someone in a *kicking* race, I'll jump on it real fast.

RODGERS:

Primarily, how I feel in relation to the weather, the competition, how far I've to go, etc. Occasionally, I think about inspirational thoughts to help me race harder. Sometimes, of course, negative thoughts enter, and then I try to be practical in overcoming them by focusing on the best ways to do my best and alleviate the pain/fatigue I feel.

SALAZAR:

About the race and competitors around me, how I feel, what I should do and when.

SPIVEY:

On what my body is doing, feeling. How my legs are responding, what my foot plant is doing. If it comes down to the final 100 meters, I will wonder if I can win, if the guy next to me might have a better kick. I start to get scared, then use that scared image to apply all my adrenaline to kick. I think that's why I have such an explosive kick.

STINTZI:

Two things only. How I feel physically—telling myself that I've been in this situation before, making sure I don't waste energy needlessly, etc. And—my race strategy. Should I be doing something at a given moment? Should I make my move now? Should I sit and kick?

VIRGIN:

Once the race is underway, I try to think about my technique and my position in relation to my key competition. I try to establish my position as soon as possible and make sure that my form is as close to perfect as possible.

The important thing in distance racing is to be as efficient at as fast a rate of speed as you are capable of. The only way I can maintain that fast speed and still have a good kick is to be completely efficient.

During the race I will be concentrating on how I am feeling

and what I am doing. I will be checking on my competition to monitor when I think is the time to make my move or to be aware of any offensive measures they may be employing.

QUESTION 4:

How do you deal with pain when it comes in your races?

BEARDSLEY:

I break the race down into one-mile segments and just go from one mile to the next until I start to feel better. Also, in my mental preparation before the race, I tell myself that at some point in the race I will have some pain and discomfort. By doing this, when and if it happens I'm ready for it, and can usually get through it much better.

BROWN:

I try very hard to ignore it. I know it's not easy, but you know it's going to happen in *every* distance race, so use it to your advantage. Expect the pain and remember everybody else feels just as bad or worse than you do most of the time.

DECKER:

Fatigue pain is easy—you learn to deal with it in training. Injury pain is a warning signal—to be careful, or else . . .

DICKERSON:

I try to prepare for this type of pain by experiencing this type of stress and pain in workouts. If you're properly trained, the pain in a race should be no worse than what you've experienced in training sessions.

DICKSON:

When I am running a good race near the lead, I feel little pain. What I do feel is usually ignored because this pain means I am running a good race. During a poor race the pain is much greater because it is much more noticeable. In this case, I try and get back into the flow of the race to forget the pain.

145

DURKIN:

Sometimes poorly, sometimes with great success. The actual pain encountered in a race is not cumulatively as bad as that experienced in practice, unless you are not in shape. Urging yourself to stay relaxed is the biggest way. You can go two ways with the same pain—grimace and thrash about and let everyone know you are in the tank. Or strive to keep good form, breathe deeply and rhythmically, keep the stride length and knee lift, and carry it off as if you are in control—because you are!

Also, pain sometimes hits you early in a race, not just the last portion. In that case you have to break the race down into segments that you deal with. In a mile, if you feel awful at the 880 mark—focus on the next quarter—try to relax and get through it—forget about the kick—your mind won't let you imagine kicking hard the last 220 when you're dead at the half! So you try to relax and break the race down into segments that you know you can run. "I know I can get to the homestretch again—then I'll see how I feel." There's pain for everyone. You just handle it without making too much of it.

GREGOREK:

First off, I hope like hell that there won't be any. It always seems that your best races didn't involve too much pain. When that pain comes, though, again I try to relax all the parts of my body. I try to hook up with others in the race and run along with them for a while trying to relax. Also I tell myself to expect some pain and know that where I'm heading and what I want is worth it all.

HILL:

Tom Byers once told me that the pain of living with yourself after a poor effort is much worse than any pain which might be experienced during a race. I would tend to agree.

LACY:

I'm not sure I deal with pain successfully. Once I begin to *dwell* on pain, the race is going to be a disaster. If I can concentrate on the race without dwelling on the pain (if there is pain), I'll be all right. But once the pain becomes over-powering, or I start to con-

146

centrate on the pain rather than the race, it becomes very difficult to forget about it.

LODWICK:

I accept it as part of the race; if one is to do his best, it'll hurt some. I realize that it is only temporary.

PADILLA:

That's a tough question. Each person is different and what works for one may be difficult for another. I guess your determination to succeed must be stronger than the pain.

Pain is interesting. It can be overcome. I've found that a race that is near my physical limit is easier than a race that is a little off my limit. In the first, I'm aware of the pain almost from the start, but I'm concentrating on the race and so the pain is pushed to the back of my mind. In a race that's a little slower, I'm not concentrating that hard, and thus I'm much more aware of the pain. The latter is more difficult to run, though you recover much faster than after the former. I believe it's all a matter of how important it is to you.

SALAZAR:

I tell myself that since I've prepared myself so well, everyone else must feel just as bad or worse, so I should hold on. I remind myself that I've felt the same many times before and that it will soon be over. Then I'll probably regret not having pushed harder.

SPIVEY:

I try to put it out of my mind—or breathe deeper to remove it. If a leg pain (cramp) comes, I know the race is nearly over for me, so I try and hang on to the finish. When situations like this arise, my legs (the calves) will hurt for three to seven days after the race, unless I put ice on them right after the race.

STINTZI:

I know that it is necessary and nothing new if I have been running hard in practice and that it is something everyone else in the race is also feeling, probably at the same time.

Everything else being equal, the person who can "run through" pain most successfully, will probably be the one who ends up winning. I don't think it is enough to try and forget about pain. You have to deal with it directly; you run in spite of the way you feel.

Pain in a race should never be something new to you. You should have felt it long ago in practice.

VIRGIN:

In regard to the pain, I try to think of it in terms of fatigue. Actually, I feel much more relieved once the fatigue starts to settle in because I know then what I have to deal with. I try to focus my attention on my form, technique, and my will to float over the terrain that I am covering. I try to think like a sleek cat running over the open prairie. When I make my moves during the race I try to envision as much power as possible. I try to accept the fatigue and pain and try to quell the inner panic that starts to begin when the legs and lungs start burning. The main thing I find is that I must concentrate on technique to get through the state of fatigue. I try to think about the finish of the race which is my objective. Sometimes I will tune out my environment, sometimes I will tune it in. I think sometimes the crowd out there helps me ignore the pain that is nagging at my body. I think it all depends on the situation. I don't face the same challenges or use the same technique in every race.

This discussion gives us a look at the psychological considerations made by the top distance runners. Their remarks suggest many helpful tips about race psychology. Several common themes emerge from their answers:

1. *Training*. Typically, the elite racer places great stock in the physical training he has done. It is a strong indicator to him of how he will race. He draws his confidence from his training. Every problem, every stress has been met there.

2. *Planning*. He plans his race carefully. He has goals and objectives for the race. He analyzes his opponents. He tries to foresee many possible happenings.

3. *Imagination*. He runs the race through in his mind beforehand. He may simulate the race in his training sessions also. He tries to imagine just how the race will *feel*.

148

4. *Diversions*. He has a set time when he plans his race, and once he's done planning it, he lets it be. He does other things which take his mind off the race. He spends his time before a race relaxing.

5. *Ritual*. He prepares the *same* way every time. His arriving at the meet, his warming-up is a set ritual. It has a stabilizing, calming effect.

6. *Challenge*. Typically, the elite racer sees nervousness as a good thing, something he has sought, and something that will benefit his race. He sees the race as a challenge and something to enjoy. His attitude is to "seize the moment."

7. *Thoughts*. The content of his thoughts and emotions is positive. He trusts himself. He evokes a positive self-image. He might think inspirational thoughts.

8. *Association*. During the race, when he thinks, his thinking is focused on how he feels, what his splits are, how the race and his strategy are evolving, and what his opponents are doing.

9. *Delicate Balance*. He speaks of trying to maintain the "fine line" between keeping his running rhythm and relaxation and efficiency—and at the same time, generating the fastest pace possible.

10. *Segmenting*. He also speaks of breaking the race into segments. He tackles one phase of the race at a time, rather than seeing it as a whole.

11. *Pain*. He is practical-minded and unsentimental about pain. He ignores it, or he tries to relax through it. Or he attends to it directly. He knows everyone in the race will feel it, and he knows they will feel as bad or worse. He also knows how subjective pain is—often the better his race, the less pain he feels.

12. *Psyching-up*. No one mentioned it. These racers emphasized keeping calm and cool.

CHAPTER SEVEN

Taking Your Act on the Road: A Mental Training Program

I ran a race recently in some awful weather. One of those gray, beginning-of-winter days, a cold, incessant drizzle interrupted only by gusts of chilling wind. A day when you hate to strip off your sweat clothes at the start. A group of us racers stood at the line until the last moment and then shed our raingear. Shivering, we waited for the gun. But the race director first wanted to explain the course. He reminded us there were two loops to run. He described each turn. We shook our arms and milled around nervously. The rain came down harder, soaking our jerseys. The director detailed the finish line procedures. He outlined his scoring system. We jogged in place miserably. The wind gusted and slapped at us. The director then itemized his starting instructions. At that point the mob turned angry. "Shoot the gun, dammit! Let's get going!"

It's time to get going and hit the roads with a mental training program. Previous chapters have given the why's and wherefore's of psychological preparation and have described specific strategies. This chapter will tie together these specifics and bring some shape to a training routine. In providing a clearer picture of the whole, several resources will be explained which will help you design and implement the best program for you.

You can set up a mental conditioning program and follow through on it the same way you would a schedule of running workouts. There are three fronts on which you can move. First, you can *assess your ability* as a runner. Construct an accurate portrait of the runner you are, the runner you want to be, and the runner you can be. The clearer this picture is, the more confident you'll be. Second, you can get in the habit of *examining your workouts and races.* Quality observation means keeping thorough records of your workouts and races. Third, these activities will pave the way to the main goal: *implementing the right psychological strategies to profit your racing.* You can incorporate mental training techniques into a schedule that is practical and effective.

ASSESSING YOUR ABILITY

The art of any sport entails learning many component skills. As you learn a sport and progress in it, it helps to be aware of the skills you do well and those you need to work on. Taking an inventory is a good, systematic way to achieve this awareness.

Assessing yourself in the skills that comprise running and racing will point up your strengths. It will show your progress and help motivate you. It will show the areas you need to emphasize. And it will help remind you of any factors you may have forgotten.

The Running Skills Inventory on the following pages lists the ingredients important to running in four categories: physical preparation; mental preparation; racing; and personal attributes. The Inventory calls for you to give yourself a rating—1 to 10—based on how accomplished you feel you are. To rate yourself in a skill, just consider this question: What percentage of the time do I perform this skill perfectly? "1" equals 10 percent of the time, "9" equals 90 percent of the time, and so on.

Give the Inventory a try. The more honest you are, the more telling this profile will be. And remember, the goal here is self-awareness, so assume a nonjudgmental attitude.

RUNNING SKILLS INVENTORY

I. *Physical Preparation*	*Circle one number*
* Using long, slow distance	1 2 3 4 5 6 7 8 9 10
* Using fast distance	1 2 3 4 5 6 7 8 9 10
* Using interval work	1 2 3 4 5 6 7 8 9 10
* Using repeats	1 2 3 4 5 6 7 8 9 10
* Using fartlek	1 2 3 4 5 6 7 8 9 10

	Circle one number
* Using hill work	1 2 3 4 5 6 7 8 9 10
* Using sprint work	1 2 3 4 5 6 7 8 9 10
* Using simulation drills	1 2 3 4 5 6 7 8 9 10
* Using stretching	1 2 3 4 5 6 7 8 9 10
* Using bounding drills	1 2 3 4 5 6 7 8 9 10
* Using weightlifting	1 2 3 4 5 6 7 8 9 10
* Using twice-a-day running	1 2 3 4 5 6 7 8 9 10
* Using other supplemental sports	1 2 3 4 5 6 7 8 9 10
* Improving aerobic endurance	1 2 3 4 5 6 7 8 9 10
* Improving anaerobic strength	1 2 3 4 5 6 7 8 9 10
* Improving sprint speed	1 2 3 4 5 6 7 8 9 10
* Pacing yourself	1 2 3 4 5 6 7 8 9 10
* Breathing control	1 2 3 4 5 6 7 8 9 10
* Running form	1 2 3 4 5 6 7 8 9 10
* Peaking at the proper time	1 2 3 4 5 6 7 8 9 10
* Using proper diet	1 2 3 4 5 6 7 8 9 10
* Getting sufficient sleep	1 2 3 4 5 6 7 8 9 10
* Selecting the right shoes	1 2 3 4 5 6 7 8 9 10
* Tending to injuries	1 2 3 4 5 6 7 8 9 10

II. *Mental Preparation* *Circle one number*

	Circle one number
* Knowing the rules of the sport	1 2 3 4 5 6 7 8 9 10
* Knowing types of training, their uses, effects	1 2 3 4 5 6 7 8 9 10
* Drawing on sources of advice, information	1 2 3 4 5 6 7 8 9 10
* Using a relaxation technique	1 2 3 4 5 6 7 8 9 10
* Using mental rehearsal	1 2 3 4 5 6 7 8 9 10
* Using attention exercises	1 2 3 4 5 6 7 8 9 10
* Using thought control: rational emotive therapy, positive affirmation, creative worrying	1 2 3 4 5 6 7 8 9 10
* Using audio-visuals	1 2 3 4 5 6 7 8 9 10
* Using gumption-producing strategies	1 2 3 4 5 6 7 8 9 10
* Selecting races	1 2 3 4 5 6 7 8 9 10
* Strategizing for a race	1 2 3 4 5 6 7 8 9 10
* Making goals	1 2 3 4 5 6 7 8 9 10
* Evaluating races	1 2 3 4 5 6 7 8 9 10

153

II. *Mental Preparation (continued)*   *Circle one number*
  * De-psyching   1 2 3 4 5 6 7 8 9 10
  * Using your imagination,
    problem solving   1 2 3 4 5 6 7 8 9 10
  * Controlling your moods   1 2 3 4 5 6 7 8 9 10
  * Maintaining a nonjudgmental
    attitude   1 2 3 4 5 6 7 8 9 10
  * Dealing with pain   1 2 3 4 5 6 7 8 9 10
  * Avoiding being psyched out by
    others   1 2 3 4 5 6 7 8 9 10

III. *Racing*

  * Warming up before a race   1 2 3 4 5 6 7 8 9 10
  * Warming down after a race   1 2 3 4 5 6 7 8 9 10
  * Using on-site mental
    strategies   1 2 3 4 5 6 7 8 9 10
  * Maintaining contact, drafting   1 2 3 4 5 6 7 8 9 10
  * Leading, pushing when alone   1 2 3 4 5 6 7 8 9 10
  * Hitting your desired pace   1 2 3 4 5 6 7 8 9 10
  * Implementing an effective
    strategy   1 2 3 4 5 6 7 8 9 10
  * Positioning, running in traffic   1 2 3 4 5 6 7 8 9 10
  * Waiting   1 2 3 4 5 6 7 8 9 10
  * Grabbing opportunities, taking
    risks   1 2 3 4 5 6 7 8 9 10
  * Responding to expected and
    unexpected happenings   1 2 3 4 5 6 7 8 9 10
  * Executing first half of the
    race   1 2 3 4 5 6 7 8 9 10
  * Executing second half of the
    race   1 2 3 4 5 6 7 8 9 10
  * Maintaining relaxation   1 2 3 4 5 6 7 8 9 10
  * Surging   1 2 3 4 5 6 7 8 9 10
  * Kicking   1 2 3 4 5 6 7 8 9 10
  * Racing well in all weather,
    terrain   1 2 3 4 5 6 7 8 9 10
  * Being consistent   1 2 3 4 5 6 7 8 9 10
  * Being versatile   1 2 3 4 5 6 7 8 9 10
  * Accepting and learning from
    bad races and savoring good
    races   1 2 3 4 5 6 7 8 9 10

IV. *Personal Attributes*   *Circle one number*

* Asserting yourself	1 2 3 4 5 6 7 8 9 10
* Using prudence, temperance	1 2 3 4 5 6 7 8 9 10
* Cooperating with others	1 2 3 4 5 6 7 8 9 10
* Deriving pleasure from your running	1 2 3 4 5 6 7 8 9 10
* Enjoying competition	1 2 3 4 5 6 7 8 9 10
* Holding to your commitments	1 2 3 4 5 6 7 8 9 10
* Keeping your sport in perspective	1 2 3 4 5 6 7 8 9 10
* Maintaining patience	1 2 3 4 5 6 7 8 9 10
* Maintaining interest	1 2 3 4 5 6 7 8 9 10
* Maintaining self-belief	1 2 3 4 5 6 7 8 9 10

This kind of assessment is subjective of course, and yet often very accurate and useful. If you want to add some objectivity and clarify your running profile even more, you can use an additional tool.

The Runner's Informational Profile which follows has you gather and record all the relevant facts about your running and racing. By assembling the truth about factors like your body strength, flexibility, maximal oxygen consumption, your racing history, history of injuries, and your personal records and goals, you arrive at a clearer picture of the runner you are and the runner you might be.

We are curious about what makes us tick, and the Runner's Informational Profile satisfies some of this curiosity. You may find facts you weren't aware of. You begin to learn the significance of the facts. You can see your way to more realistic expectations. You can see how you compare to where you were last year, and how you compare to others. Also, this Profile aids coaches and others who wish to help you in your running.

Some clinics will help you gather the medical facts pertinent to your running. For example, the Sports Medicine Athletic Rehabilitation and Training Clinic in Cupertino, California, provides a battery of diagnostic tests analyzing your physical state. The test results are later presented to you in a 35-page book, a medical profile with facts in ten different categories.[1]

You can, however, ascertain most of the pertinent facts about your physical state on your own and for free by using the Runner's Informational Profile which follows on these pages. The indices that are footnoted refer you to methods for easy self-testing. The few indices that are starred are ones requiring equipment you probably wouldn't have. For these, consult your local high school or college physical education department or your local health club. They'll have the equipment.

RUNNER'S INFORMATIONAL PROFILE

Your Running History

1. How many years (months) have you been running?
2. How regularly do you train?
3. How much time do you have available to run?
4. How many miles per week do you run?
5. What kind(s) of training do you do?
6. How many years (months) have you been racing?
7. How frequently do you race?
8. What distances do you normally race?
9. Briefly describe the past success you've had in racing.
10. Briefly describe any pertinent athletic background of your mother, father, brothers, sisters.
11. Name your past and present coach(es).
12. What percentage of the time do you have a friend or family member watch you when you race?
13. What is your main reason for doing this sport?
14. What things motivate you in your running?

Physical Facts

15. Height
16. Weight
17. *Percent fat[2]
18. Age
19. Resting pulse
20. Maximal heart rate[3]
21. *Blood pressure

22. *Maximum oxygen consumption[4]
23. *Lung capacity[5]
24. Flexibility[6]
25. Agility[7]
26. Vertical jump[8]
27. Sixty seconds of sit-ups
28. *Bench press[9]
29. "Flying fifty"[10]

Running Form Analysis[11]

30. Which aspects of your running style do you do well?
    (foot placement; leg carriage; arm carriage; position of body and head)
31. Which aspects of your running style do you need to improve?
    (foot placement; leg carriage; arm carriage; position of body and head)

History of Injuries, Illnesses

32. What injuries have you had? How long before you were back to 100 percent? What therapy was used?
33. Any recurring injuries?
34. Any current aches and pains?
35. Podiatric check (orthotics needed? leg length difference? shoe wear? blisters?)
36. What illnesses have you had? Duration, antidote used?
37. Any recurring illnesses?
38. Allergies?
39. Any other special problems?

Running Skills Inventory

40. List the skills in which you scored yourself 1, 2, or 3. (see pages 152–155) In other words, the ones you need to work on.
    Physical preparation: _____
    Mental preparation: _____
    Racing: _____
    Personal attributes: _____
41. Other Sports Profiles[12]

Goals

Event	Current Personal Record	Mid-Season Goal	End-of-Season Goal	Ultimate Goal
42.				
43.				
44.				
45.				
46.				
47.				
48. Describe your non-time goals.				

Racing

49. Write a description of your "Best Race Ever" or your "Perfect Race Feeling."
50. Describe the things you do and the conditions under which you race best.

Additional Comments

Once a year you can do the Running Skills Inventory and the Runner's Informational Profile. And you can do something more frequently which will also add greatly to your self-knowledge: Keep records of your training sessions and your races.

SCRUTINIZING YOUR WORKOUTS AND RACES

Pilots keep logs. Surgeons keep journals. Where quality performance is essential, careful records are kept. Most serious runners keep training diaries. A diary helps you see patterns. Logging in the facts of your daily performance helps you plan, compare, diagnose, and modify. It helps you see the forest through the trees.

"My diary taught me almost all I know of running," says *Runner's World* editor Joe Henderson. "It showed me what I ran, how to run better, how to think about what I'd run. . . . So much of what runners do is invisible, gone behind us as soon as we pick up our feet, that we need this reminder of where we've been and what we did there. . . . The trick in turning your history into a better future is learning to read that trail. Where on it did you move easily and quickly? What wrong turns did you take?"[13]

Being naturally compulsive, many runners are hard-core log-keepers. Bill Rodgers knows what he's run everyday for eighteen years. Joe Henderson has kept his diary since November 1959.

You can choose from several different kinds of running diaries today in the bookstores, or you can design your own. Below is a sample page from the training log I recommend. I include it here because most diaries lack one important notation—a place to write about the mental training you did that day. Without this notation, mental training is too easily relegated to an afterthought and then forgotten.

A few tips about using a training log. It should be simple, fast, and easy to use, otherwise you won't keep it going. Use it daily. Some of the notations, such as weight and pulse, you should take under the same conditions each day. That way you'll have proper comparisons. See page 160 *The Competitive Edge* Training Log.

A post-race scenario: You find out the time you ran. You think: "All right! Good race!" or "Damn! Bad race." You put on your sweats and jog down. Briefly, in your mind, you play a round of "I felt good when I . . ." or "I should have . . ." or "I ran bad because . . ." As you leave the race site, you're already planning the next day's workout. "I need to do more of . . ."

Most runners spend little time, if any, considering the race they've just run. And that's ironic—whereas they'll record their training, they'll keep no records examining the very thing they're training for. If it's a bad race, they want to forget about it as soon as possible. If it's a good race, they don't want to spoil the "magic" of it by thinking about it. These are the runners who then make the same mistakes in races, never seeing the relevant connections and significances in their race behavior.

THE COMPETITIVE EDGE TRAINING LOG

	Monday	Tuesday	Wednesday	Thursday	Friday	Saturday	Sunday
RESTING PULSE							
WEIGHT							
HOURS OF PREVIOUS NIGHT'S SLEEP							
RUNNING WORKOUT KIND							
DISTANCE							
DURATION							
SITE CONDITIONS							
QUALITY RATING							
MENTAL TRAINING							
KIND							
DURATION							
QUALITY RATING							
OTHER SUPPLEMENTAL ACTIVITIES							
ACHES, PAINS							
COMMENTS:							

This attitude flies in the face of all we've said about sound mental preparation. Setting aside time after your race for some careful evaluation helps reinforce the things you did well and enables you to learn from your mistakes.

The Race Evaluation below can aid you in your race analysis. Some of the notations on it may be done beforehand. Most can and should be done soon after your race. Make your evaluating brief and direct. Don't dwell on the bad parts of your race, and keep in mind the good aspects of it.

RACE EVALUATION

1. Name of race
2. Date, starting time
3. Location
4. Distance
5. Competition
6. Weeks (months) since last race
7. Weather and course conditions
8. Goals (time and non-time)
9. Race strategy; and possible mishaps and contingencies
10. Mental preparation strategy
11. Duration of warm-up _____ Duration of
    warm-down _____
12. Pulse on starting line
    Arousal level (Assess your A.L.: 1 to 10, "1" being nearly falling asleep and "10" being hysterical)
13. Finish time
14. Place
15. Splits
16. Things I did well in the race
17. Things I need to work on
18. Performance rating (1–10). How close did I come to what I was capable of running that day?
19. Mentally playback the best parts of the race.
    Check here _____.
    Watch a film or videotape of the race. Check here _____.
20. Other comments about the race.

IMPLEMENTING A MENTAL TRAINING PROGRAM

As you assess yourself and as you examine your workouts and races, you'll come to have a better idea of which psychological aspects you need to work on. You'll be able to implement your mental training program with much more purpose. In previous chapters we've described several mental training strategies. The chart below will help you organize the various possibilities. Each technique has a specific use.

Don't try learning them all at once. Tackling many at once just overloads your computer. Give yourself time to learn, feel comfortable with, and know the effectiveness of one at a time.

Think of your psychological workout as you would your running workout. Many of the same principles apply. Consistency, for example. Arrange a convenient time and place to practice regularly. As in running, consistency is more important than the time and effort you put in.

Gradualism is another principle you can apply to mental training. Initially, spend only five to ten minutes on a technique. As you improve and see the results, and as your motivation for this training grows, your sessions may expand to fifteen, twenty, or thirty minutes. You'll eventually be able to incorporate several strategies into your schedule. The hard-day/easy-day concept applies also. A quality mental training session takes emotional energy, so give yourself an easy day, or a day off, before you try another high-intensity session.

A MENTAL TRAINING PROGRAM

Training Technique	Description	Chapter Reference	Goal	Frequency
Relaxation technique	using a technique such as progressive relaxation to calm your body	3	to thoroughly relax your body at will under any pressure	weekly or more often
Mental rehearsal	visualizing the race in detail to rehearse and program perfect performance	4	to attain greater vividness; to embed more deeply perfect race programs	weekly or more often
Attention exercises	using drills to improve attentional focus	4	to widen and narrow your attention appropriately; to become distraction-proof	weekly
Thought control: rational emotive therapy, positive affirmation, creative worrying, etc.	disciplining your thoughts, repeating ones which will help you keep things in perspective, build a strong self-image, and purge worries	4,5	to gain strong habits of mind; to engage in thinking that is energizing	on-going

A MENTAL TRAINING PROGRAM

Training Technique	Description	Chapter Reference	Goal	Frequency
Gumption-producing strategies	doing and thinking things which increase emotional energy	5	to become an expert at regulating and building emotional energy	on-going
Simulations	workouts designed to be much like some aspect you'll face in the race	4	to be able to handle any race difficulty because you've re-hearsed them all repeatedly	weekly
Audio-visuals	using tapes, films, photos to evoke positive associations and emotions for the race	4	to build and use an AV library that works for you	weekly
Race study: race selection, strategizing, goal-making, post-race evaluation	bringing your analytical powers to bear in race planning	4,5,7	to become a master at sizing up your races	before and after each race

A MENTAL TRAINING PROGRAM

Training Technique	Description	Chapter Reference	Goal	Frequency
De-psyching	keeping your activities and thoughts completely away from running	4,5	to become adept at shutting off running so your batteries can recharge	before and after each race
On-site arousal strategies	employing calming techniques (or bracing) to achieve the right level of arousal at race time	3	to become an expert at knowing your optimal arousal level and attaining it at race time	before each race
Recency coding	visualizing the best parts of your race afterwards	4	to store and embed strong, clear images of your best racing	after each race

A MENTAL TRAINING PROGRAM

We've all seen hundreds of workout schedules. What might a mental training schedule look like? Here's a sample:

Monday	Tuesday	Wednesday	Thursday	Friday	Saturday	Sunday
* race study and * audio-visuals	* relaxation technique and * attention exercises or thought control	* race simu-lations during workout	* relaxa-tion technique and * mental rehearsal	* de-psyching	race day: * on-site strategies * and after, * recency coding and race evaluation	* de-psyching
10–30 minutes	10–30 minutes	10–30 minutes	10–30 minutes		10–30 minutes	

How can you tell whether your mental training program is working? What signs of improvement can you look for? Here are several questions you can ask yourself:

* Are you less uptight before races?
* Are your races better than your workouts?
* Are you able to race better in big races?
* Are you racing closer to your perceived potential? Do you feel you are able to draw everything out of yourself in your races?
* Do you compete better?
* Are you more responsive and spontaneous in races?
* Are you taking more risks in races?
* Are you enjoying the sport more?

CHAPTER EIGHT

The Future of Footracing: Limits?

By the year 2000, top milers will cover their distance in under 3:40. Before the year 2050, a very fit individual will break the 3:30 barrier. In the marathon by the year 2050, the elite will average less than 4:30 per mile, finishing in under two hours. The de Castellas and Salazars of today would be left gasping, nearly two miles behind.

Tom Osler, author of *The Serious Runner's Handbook* (1978), has made a study of distance races, plotting all the record performances since the 1800s and designing a logarithmic scale by which you can compare and predict times. Olser found that record times over the years have come in a steady, almost orderly way. "Naturally, there must be some limit beyond which man cannot go," says Osler. "That limit however, appears to be far, far in the future. Track performances have improved at the rate of one-half second per mile per year since 1920. The rate has not declined for fifty years. We can expect, therefore, that the present records are still far from the ultimate in human potential."[1]

Distance records fell in a blizzard the last two years— Coe's 3:47.33 mile; Moorcroft's 13:00.42 five thousand meters; Salazar's 2:08.13 marathon and Joan Benoit's 2:22.26. These times were big improvements, yet as impressive as they are, they fall right in line with Osler's predictions for the 1980s.

Some take issue with predictions such as Osler's, saying the limits to running achievements are close. Dr. David Costill points out there may be physical limits of how much workout stress an elite runner can add to his regimen. "When you run that high intensity and pound the ground, the trauma to the musculature is pheno-

169

menal, so maybe our chance for full development of runners is limited because of environmental conditions, gravitational problems, G forces."[2]

Then there are those who foresee a future different from both Osler and Costill. Herb Elliott is one. In the 1950s Elliott lopped four seconds off the mile record and in so doing, convinced everyone the four-minute mark was no ultimate barrier. Predicts Elliott: "There's probably going to be a quantum leap forward when we understand our minds better. I believe that we just barely understand our physical capabilities at this stage of the game. There will come a time when knowledge of ourselves will enable us to tap that physical resource. At that time, we'll see a quantum leap in all sports . . . I see three minutes as a possibility, but not with our current knowledge."[3]

Dr. Vaughan Thomas also speaks of quantum leaps. Thomas is a well-known British coach, former national champion in track and cycling, and an author-lecturer. In *Science and Sport: How to Measure and Improve Athletic Performance*, Dr. Thomas conjectures: "It is conceivable that men will, during the next million years, achieve the power of telekinesis, making it possible for them to transfer their bodies from one place to another instantaneously."[4]

Whimsical ideas, yes. But understand that Thomas and forecasters like him believe we have only just scratched the surface in learning how to train the mind. Dr. Barbara Brown, author of *Supermind—The Ultimate Energy*, puts it like this: "The ways we now search for the mother lode of mind, like self-hypnosis or imagery or T.M., may well be as crude and chancey as those of the old gold-rush muleteers with their heavy picks and leak sieves."[5] These forecasters believe once we learn how to unleash the mind's awesome potential, anything will be possible.

LOOKING FOR A FEW GOOD ATHLETES?

Already people have given us glimpses into this awesome potential. There is Ramanand Yogi, for example. After years of yoga discipline, this master could wield uncanny mental power over his bodily functions. In one demonstration he remained in a sealed

170

box for over ten hours. His ability to radically decrease his oxygen consumption allowed him to do this. At one point, he lowered his oxygen consumption to 25 percent of the minimum level scientists believe necessary to sustain life.[6]

There are the lung-gom-pa, Tibetan monks whose running prowess is legendary. The lung-gom-pa reportedly travel through mountainous terrain to villages hundreds of miles away, running nonstop for days. These feats of endurance are achieved in a trance state. The lung-gom-pa have a curious form of training. They do no running. Their training consists of meditating in secluded cubicles for years.[7]

Another athlete extraordinaire is Morihei Uyeshiba, a martial arts master. Uyeshiba developed several amazing abilities. Had there not been reliable witnesses at his demonstrations, he would have been discounted as a hoax. In one such demonstration, Uyeshiba allowed two attackers to charge him. With seemingly no chance of escape, Uyeshiba was suddenly out of their way, facing the two colliding men. A film taken of the incident shows frame by frame the steady, sequential, on-rush of the attackers. Of the master, in two consecutive frames, it shows a motionless, trapped Uyeshiba facing the charge in one frame, and Uyeshiba several feet away in the other frame—a seemingly impossible jump verified on the uncut film. Witnesses claim that on another occasion, Uyeshiba, encircled by weaponed attackers, disappeared and then reappeared in the same moment at the top of a stairway.[8] Dr. Thomas's prediction of telekinesis come true?

ON THE DIFFICULTIES OF GRASPING SMOKE

The mind is a dominant force in any athlete's life and it monitors his every motion, controls his every emotion, allows him superlative productions one night, damns him to embarrassing incompetence the next. It is whimsical, ornery, unpredictable, fractious, inconsistent, easily influenced, controlled with difficulty, and a friend only to those who have attained superiority at their jobs. It is regarded with clichés and surrounded by an aura of mysticism; it is wooed, courted, and pampered, and called many names by many people in many fields. An understanding of it is as difficult as an understanding of a child's dream, a grasping of it is as elusive as the grasping of smoke hanging over a crowded bar, yet it is never ignored, it is continually considered. It, too, must be conditioned, like the body, and as with the body, this does not happen quickly or easily.[9]

Marty Liquori
On the Run—In Search of the Perfect Race

Liquori reminds us the relationship the runner has with the mind-side of his sport is tenuous. In our optimism about the prospects of mental conditioning, it's good to remember it "does not happen quickly or easily." Developing mental skills may not be quite as hard as "the grasping of smoke," but it certainly will demand a lot of patience and hard work.

Training for mental skills, the runner will face several difficulties. The newcomer will have to deal with bias: "Mental training is weird" and "You're not really *doing* anything when you do it."

Mental training may mean more time spent training, which the runner is reluctant to spend because his time is already so consumed by running, stretching, and weight lifting and unlike running where partners can make the training more fun and interesting, mental training will always be a solitary activity.

Transference of mental skills from the quiet of a room to the pressure of a crowded stadium will always pose a challenge. The athlete has this dilemma: The more he desires his goal, the more arousal he'll have to face.

By its nature, the outcome of mental training will be less tangible and less immediate. A series of good workouts may give you a definite feeling of increased strength in your legs. What you "get" from mental rehearsal will be less palpable.

Many physical factors enter into producing a good race, thus complicating the sport, and when you add the important psychological factors, you have a task that is slippery indeed.

Harry Groves, the highly successful track and cross-country coach at Penn State University, spoke at a recent track clinic of the difficulty of controlling the psychological component in racing. Groves related a story about a psychologist friend with whom he jogged. Often he and Groves would discuss the psychological as-

172

pects of distance racing. Groves, like most of us, had much respect and appreciation for the psychologist's insights in these matters. At the end of one track season, Groves had a top runner who had posted a fine 10,000 meter time. Groves was priming him for the NCAA Championships in June. In May the runner's time was one of the best in the nation. All was smooth-sailing and optimism. But three weeks later the young man ran miserably and failed to make it to the Nationals. Shortly thereafter, Groves saw his psychologist friend, and with embarrassment, told the story of his runner's "psych-out." Groves explained to his clinic audience his relief when the psychologist could only shrug and commiserate: "Yeah, just the way it is, huh?"[10]

Gaining control of both physical and mental parts of racing, difficult as it is, is worth the effort. Mental skills, as we've shown in this book, can be acquired in a methodical way through practice and can greatly enhance performance. Knowledge of sports psychology is in place and awaits implementation by coaches and athletes. And what better practitioners! Many coaches, intuitive and pragmatic, are already pretty good practicing psychologists. And for many athletes, who already have a talent for being in tune with the body, it is a small step to apply that talent to getting in tune with the mind.

If this book has started you thinking about the mental aspects of your sport, then it has achieved part of its purpose; but only part, because the main purpose comes not in just thinking, but in *doing*. No skill was ever attained by reading a book. So give the techniques a try. If you implement just one, you'll be ahead.

The future of athletic performance is sports psychology. The next great advances in running and all sports will be based on it.

"NOW ENTERTAIN CONJECTURE
OF A TIME WHEN . . ."

In the future, distance racers will wear shoes that are highly shock-absorbent and nearly weightless and someone will discover a training system which allows runners to put more stress on their legs without breaking them down.

173

Each day before their workout, runners may take a quick and simple blood analysis and muscle fiber test. Then, after logging the data into their personal computer, plus information about their diet, sleep, and pulse rate, they'll receive a printout of their optimal workout for the day.

In the future, runners will train almost injury-free. The few injuries they get, they'll get rid of quickly thanks to advances in sports medicine.

When the runners go to the track, they'll train on special surfaces so well-tuned that running will be like taking off lead boots. Stride length and cadence will effortlessly increase.

But these external improvements, as dramatic as they'll be, will ultimately lead to diminishing returns—while improvements in the inner side of athletics will be shaking and rearranging the entire landscape of sport, thrusting it to a new plain.

In the future, time spent in physical training will shrink, and time spent in psychological preparation will grow. Like Eastern masters in the martial arts, the older athletes will excel.

Top runners will be geniuses in controlling "involuntary" functions. In training, perhaps, they'll use "on-board" computers to get feedback on oxygen consumption, blood flow, glycogen depletion, respiration, and brain waves, helping them learn optimal relaxed concentration.

They'll be sophisticates of psychic energy. They'll become as adept at regulating the ebb and flow of their emotional fuel as they are at regulating their race pace.

In the future, before a race, runners may sit before a screen—with a machine monitoring their brain patterns—and they will watch their own race, rehearse it, create it themselves as they visualize it.

The top runners will keep a large staff busy making daily changes in the record books.

One situation will remain the same—one person will win the race. Behind him, undoubtedly some of the old frustration will exist—to run, say, 3:31 for the mile and finish last! But the difference will be that this last-place finisher will know he brought out the very best he had that day.

And what will this future mean to us ordinary runners?

174

For all of us it will offer a channel to the extraordinary potential within. It will mean the joy of going faster and farther.

Personal bests will come steadily. Our unschooled former rivals will be left in the dust. We'll race better than we work out. And we'll race better, the bigger the race.

Mental training will mean greater control of our emotional states—and with that control, greater confidence in all our pursuits.

This future will mean fewer scenes of post-race regrets, self-accusations, and fist-pounding.

It will mean more moments of reckless abandon, of holy spontaneity, of arms raised at the finish.

Notes

CHAPTER ONE

[1]Pat Putnam, "Track and Field," *Sports Illustrated*, March 13, 1972, p. 57.

[2]Tex Maule, "Jim Ryun: Starting Over," *Runner*, July 1981, p. 36.

[3]Putnam, *op. cit.*, p. 57.

[4]Marty Liquori and Skip Myslenski, *On the Run—In Search of the Perfect Race* (New York: William Morrow, 1979), p. 205.

[5] Amby Burfoot, "Exclusive Interview—Frank Shorter," *Runner's World*, July 1982, p. 26.

[6]Thomas A. Tutko and Umberto Tosi, *Sports Psyching: Playing Your best Game All of the Time* (Los Angeles: J. P. Tarcher, 1976), pp. 9–10.

[7]Burfoot, *op. cit.*, p. 27.

[8]Robert M. Nideffer, *The Inner Athlete: Mind Plus Muscle for Winning* (New York: Thomas Crowell, 1976), p. 5.

[9]Tutko and Tosi, *op. cit.*, p. 3.

[10]Richard Suinn, "Body Thinking: Psychology for Olympic Champs," *Psychology Today*, July 1976, pp. 38–43.

[11]Ivan Berenyi, "Meet the World's Best Marathoner," *Runner*, Jan. 1981, pp. 65–67.

[12]Jim Kaplan, "He's Off in a Zone of His Own," *Sports Illustrated*, August 30, 1982, pp. 48–51.

[13]Pam Wing, "Man as Marine Mammal," *Oceans*, March 1981, pp. 26–27.

CHAPTER TWO

[1]David L. Costill, *A Scientific Approach to Distance Running* (Los Altos, California: Track and Field News Press, 1979) p. 10.

[2]William Sheldon, *Varieties of Human Physique* (New York: Harper, 1940).

³Costill, *op. cit.*, p. 34.

⁴George Sheehan, *Running and Being* (New York: Simon and Schuster, 1978), p. 32.

⁵*Ibid.*, pp. 32–34.

⁶Cliff Temple, "A Nice Bloke Breaks Through," *Runner*, October 1982, p. 45.

⁷Tutko and Tosi, *op. cit.*, p. 36.

⁸Craig A. Fisher, ed., *Psychology of Sport* (Palo Alto, California: Mayfield Publishing, 1976), p. 136.

⁹*Ibid.*, pp. 119–120.

¹⁰*Ibid.*, p. 121.

¹¹Nideffer, *op. cit.*, p. 86.

¹²*Ibid.*, p. 77.

¹³Fisher, *op. cit.*, p. 160.

¹⁴Billy Squires, *Improving Your Running* (Lexington, Massachusetts: Stephen Green, 1982) pp. 170–171.

CHAPTER THREE

¹Bud Winter, *Relax and Win* (San Diego: A. S. Barnes, 1981), pp. XI–XIV.

²*Ibid.*, p. 241.

³Hal Higdon, "Loosen Up and Fly Right," *Runner*, May 1983, p. 36.

⁴Tom Osler, *Serious Runner's Handbook* (Mountain View, California: Anderson World, 1978), p. 49.

⁵Nideffer, *op. cit.*, pp. 160–161.

⁶Herbert Benson, *The Relaxation Response* (New York: William Morrow, 1975), pp. 100–101.

⁷*Ibid.*, p. 25.

⁸Rainer Martens, in conversation, Champaign, Illinois, October 1982.

⁹Higdon, *op. cit.*, pp. 37–38.

CHAPTER FOUR

[1]Michael Murphy and Rhea A. White, *The Psychic Side of Sports* (Reading, Massachusetts: Addison Wesley, 1978), p. 85.

[2]Roger Bannister, *The Four-Minute Mile* (New York: Dodd, Mead, 1955), pp. 213–214.

[3]Sheehan, *op. cit.*, p. 174.

[4]Barbara B. Brown, *Supermind: The Ultimate Energy* (New York: Harper and Row, 1980), p. 56.

[5]Ken Moore, "The Olympics," *Sports Illustrated*, August 4, 1980, p. 16.

[6]William P. Morgan, "The Mind of the Marathoner," *Psychology Today*, April 1978, p. 39 and p. 45.

[7]Jim Stintzi, survey response: See Chapter Six—"What the Experts Say."

[8]Don Swartz with Ron Wayne, "How to Mentally Prepare for Better Performances," *Runner's World*, November 1979, p. 93.

[9]Hanns Maier, "Seko," *Runner's World*, June 1981, pp. 45–46.

[10]Timothy W. Gallwey, *The Inner Game of Tennis* (New York: Random House, 1976) p. 31.

[11]Robert Singer, "Thought Processes and Emotions in Sport," *Physician and Sports Medicine*, July 1982, p. 81.

[12]Eugene Herrigel, *Zen in the Art of Archery* (New York: Pantheon Books, 1953) p. vii.

[13]Michael H. Sacks and Michael L. Sachs, ed., *Psychology of Running* (Champaign, Illinois: Human Kinetics, 1981), pp. 171–172.

[14]Robert Singer, *Myths and Truths in Sports Psychology* (New York: Harper and Row, 1975), p. 68.

[15]William Morgan, in conversation, Madison, Wisconsin, July 1982.

[16]Jerry Lynch, "Positive Thinking," *Runner*, July 1982, p. 23.

[17]Jim Lilliefors, *The Running Mind* (Mountain View, California: Anderson World, 1978), p. 68.

[18]Janet Pactor-Azor, *Optimizing Athletic Performance With Biofeedback Training*, report from Princeton Biofeedback Clinic, Princeton, New Jersey, 1980.

[19]Steven DeVore and Greggory DeVore, *Sybervision: Muscle Memory Programming for Every Sport* (Chicago: Chicago Review Press, 1980), p. 2.

[20]Maxwell Maltz, *Psycho-Cybernetics* (Englewood Cliffs, New Jersey: Prentice-Hall, 1960), p. 32.

[21]Suinn, *op. cit.*, pp. 41–43.

CHAPTER FIVE

[1]Robert M. Pirsig, *Zen and the Art of Motorcycle Maintenance* (New York: William Morrow, 1974), p. 297.

[2]*Ibid.*, p. 297.

[3]Hal Higdon, "The Shape of Things to Come," *Runner*, July 1983, p. 36.

[4]*Ibid.*, p. 36.

[5]John Gregorek, survey response: See Chapter Six—"What the Experts Say."

[6]Kenny Moore, *Best Efforts: World Class Runners and Races* (New York: Doubleday, 1982), p. 178.

[7]William F. Straub, ed., *Sports Psychology—An Analysis of Athletic Behavior* (Ithaca, New York: Movement Publications, 1978), p. 39.

[8]Pirsig, *op. cit.*, p. 304.

[9]*Runner's World Magazine, Guide To Sprinting* (Mountain View, California: World Publications, 1973), p. 3.

[10]Costill, *op. cit.*, p. 26.

[11]*Ibid.*, p. 111.

[12]Albert Ellis, *Reason and Emotion in Psychotherapy* (New York: Dodd, Meade, 1955), pp. 60–85.

[13]Pirsig, *op. cit.*, pp. 318–319.

CHAPTER SEVEN

[1]Richard Benyo, "Diagnostic Tune-Up for the Human Body," *Runner's World*, August 1981, pp. 66–75.

[2]To measure your percentage of body fat, you'll need a skinfold caliper and someone who knows how to use it. Typically, the greatest

accuracy is obtained by measuring four locations on the body: the back of upper arm, the front of upper arm, back just below shoulder blade, and the side of the waist.

[3]Maximal heart rate is commonly figured by subtracting your age from 220 (beats per minute). It's good to know your maximal heart rate because often training programs prescribe that you run at a certain percentage of your maximal heart rate.

[4]"VO$_2$ max" is one of the best indications of a distance runner's cardiovascular fitness. This reading can be obtained if you have access to a bicycle ergometer. The ergometer makes it possible for you to do an exactly quantified piece of work. Your pulse rate is taken at the completion of the work, then recovery rate is checked, your weight is figured in, and you have a VO$_2$ max reading. For further reference: Per-Olof Astrand, *Work Tests With the Bicycle Ergometer* (Varberg, Sweden M.C.B., 1982).

[5]Lung capacity, or "vital capacity," can be checked if you have access to either a dry spirometer or wet spirometer. You blow into the apparatus, emptying your lungs, and a reading is obtained.

[6]There are many tests measuring flexibility at various points of the body. For instance, to measure the flexibility of the hamstrings, the "sit and reach" test is often used, where the subject sits with legs straight (and heels up against something stationary) and then reaches forward as far as he can and touches—and the distance (from the heels) is measured. For the quadriceps, the subject stands on one leg and pulls the foreleg and heel of the other leg back toward his buttocks and measures the distance between. For further reference: John E. Beaulieu, *Stretching for all Sports* (Pasadena, California: The Athletic Press, 1980).

[7]Agility, defined as the rapidity in which body position can be changed, is also a useful reading to get and can be obtained by getting timed on any of the nationally-normed "line tests," such as the "shuttle run" or the Texas Motor Test. A good reference: Barry Johnson and Jack Nelson, *Practical Measurements for Evaluation in Physical Education* (Minneapolis: Burgess, 1969).

[8]Vertical jump is a measure of gross leg power, explosiveness, your "spring." It is easily tested by standing next to a wall, reaching and touching as high on the wall as you can, then jumping up and reaching and touching the same way—and subtracting the two measurements.

[9]Finding how much you can bench press is one way of testing upper body strength. Seeing how many dips or pull ups you can do is also useful. You can do another valuable test if you have access to any of the latest weight machines built on the Cybex principle, where you can find the

actual strength of each individual muscle group—and also get a reading on any muscle strength imbalances.

[10]A "flying fifty" is a measure of your sprint speed. Take your time for a fifty-yard dash. Use a "flying" or running start so that you test just sprinting, not starting ability.

[11]Have someone who understands (and can teach) good running form watch you run. Videotape your running and analyze it. Also it helps to study films of other runners with good form.

[12]Several useful psychological assessment tests for athletes are available, such as the Athletic Motivation Inventory (Athletic Motivation, San Mateo, California), which gives a profile of the athlete in eleven traits.

[13]Joe Henderson, "The Runner's Diary: How to Keep and Use It," *Runner's World*, August 1979, pp. 57–58.

CHAPTER EIGHT

[1]Osler, *op. cit.*, p. 171.

[2]Hal Higdon, "Man Against Myth," *Runner*, September, 1983, p. 49.

[3]Squires, *op. cit.*, pp. 167–168.

[4]Vaughn Thomas, *Science and Sport*. (Boston: Little, Brown, 1970), p. 136.

[5]Brown, *op. cit.*, 167–168.

[6]Richard M. Restak, *The Brain: The Last Frontier* (New York: Doubleday, 1979), p. 162.

[7]Murphy and White, *op. cit.*, pp. 86–88.

[8]George Leonard, *The Ultimate Athlete: Revisioning Sports, Physical Education and the Body* (New York: The Viking Press, 1975) pp. 252–253.

[9]Marty Liquori and Skip Myslenski, *On the Run—In Search of the Perfect Race* (New York: William Morrow, 1979), p. 161.

[10]Harry Groves, Indiana University Track Clinic, Bloomington, Indiana, November, 1982.

Sources Consulted

Bannister, Roger. *The Four-Minute Mile*. New York: Dodd, Mead, 1955.

Beisser, Arnold. *The Madness in Sport*. Bowie, Maryland: Charles Press, 1977.

Bennett, James G., and Pravitz, James E. *The Miracle of Sports Psychology*. Englewood Cliffs, New Jersey: Prentice-Hall, 1982.

Bensen, Herbert. *The Relaxation Response*. New York: William Morrow, 1975.

Bourne, Richard. "Hypnosis: Key to Relaxed Running." *Runner's World*, August 1978, pp. 55–57.

Brokhin, Yuri. *The Big Red Machine*. New York: Random House, 1978.

Brown, Barbara B. *Supermind: The Ultimate Energy*. New York: Harper and Row, 1980.

Burfoot, Amby. "Exclusive Interview—Frank Shorter." *Runner's World*, July, 1982, pp. 25–30.

Castaneda, Carlos. *The Teachings of Don Juan: A Yaqui Way of Knowledge*. Berkeley: University of California Press, 1968.

Costill, David L. *A Scientific Approach to Distance Running*, Los Altos, California: Track and Field News Press, 1979.

Cratty, Bryant J. *Psychology in Contemporary Sport: Guidelines for Coaches and Athletes*. Englewood Cliffs, New Jersey: Prentice-Hall, 1973.

Daniel, Mike. " 'The Choke' and What You Can Do About It." *Scholastic Coach*, October and November, 1981, pp. 70–72, and pp. 43–90.

DeVore, Steven, and DeVore, Greggory. *Sybervision: Muscle Memory Programming for Every Sport*. Chicago: Chicago Review Press, 1980.

Dunnett, William, and Williams, Jack. "Strength Through Stress." *Runner's World*, February, 1980, pp. 55–57.

Dyer, Wayne W., M.D. *Your Erroneous Zones*. New York: Funk and Wagnalls, 1976.

Ellis, Albert. *Reason and Emotion in Psychotherapy*. New York: Dodd, Mead, 1955.

Fisher, Craig A., ed. *Psychology of Sport*. Palo Alto, California: Mayfield Publishing, 1976.

Frankl, Viktor E. *Man's Search for Meaning*. New York: Simon and Schuster, 1963.

Gallwey, W. Timothy. *The Inner Game of Tennis*. New York: Random House, 1974.

——————————, *Inner Tennis—Playing the Game*. New York: Random House, 1976.

——————————, and Kriegel, Bob. *Inner Skiing*. New York: Random House, 1977.

Gilbert, Doug. *The Miracle Machine*. New York: Coward, McCann, and Geoghegan, 1980.

Green, Judith. "The Mind-Body Hyphen." *Social Policy*, March/April, 1974, pp. 38–42.

Herrigel, Eugene. *Zen in the Art of Archery*. New York: Pantheon Books. 1953.

Higdon, Hal. "Loosen Up and Fly Right." *Runner*, May, 1983, pp. 34–39.

——————————, "Man Against Myth." *Runner*, September, 1983, pp. 44–51.

Jacobson, Edmund. *Progressive Relaxation*. Chicago: University of Chicago Press, (third printing) 1974.

——————————, *You Must Relax*. New York: McGraw-Hill, 1976.

Jaynes, Julian. *The Origin of Consciousness in the Breakdown of the Bicameral Mind*. Boston: Houghton Mifflin, 1976.

Kaplan, Jim. "He's Off in a Zone of His Own." *Sports Illustrated*, August 30, 1982, pp. 48–51.

Kauss, David R. *Peak Performance*. Englewood Cliffs: New Jersey, 1980.

Kellner, Stan. *Taking It to the Limit With Basketball—Cybernetics*. West Islip, New York: Durite Printing, 1978.

Kenyon, Gerald, Ed. *Contemporary Psychology of Sport*. Washington, D.C.: Athletic Institute, 1970.

184

Kiev, Ari, M.D. "The Power of Concentration." *Nautilus Magazine*, December/January, 1983, pp. 61–62.

Klavora, Peter and Daniel, Juri V., ed. *Coach, Athlete, and the Sport Psychologist*. Champaign, IL: Human Kinetics, 1979.

Leonard, George. *The Ultimate Athlete: Re-visioning Sports, Physical Education and the Body*. New York: The Viking Press, 1975.

Lilliefors, Jim. *The Running Mind*. Mountain View, California: Anderson World, 1978.

Liquori, Marty, and Myslenski, Skip. *On the Run—In Search of the Perfect Race*. New York: William Morrow, 1979.

Lynch, Jerry. "Hitting the Wall Head First." *Runner*, January 1982, pp. 54–57, and subsequent articles in *Runner*: July, 1982; January 1983, April 1983, July 1983, December 1983; February, 1984.

McNair, Douglas M., Lorr, Maurice, and Droppleman, Leo F. *Profile of Mood States*. San Diego, California: Educational and Industrial Testing Service, 1971.

Maier, Hanns. "Seko." *Runner's World*, June, 1981, pp. 45–47.

Maltz, Maxwell. *Psycho-Cybernetics*. Englewood Cliffs, New Jersey: Prentice-Hall, 1960.

Martens, Rainer. *Sports Competition Anxiety Test*. Champaign, Illinois: Human Kinetics, 1977.

Maule, Tex. "Jim Ryun." *Runner*, July, 1981, pp. 34–42.

Millman, Dan. *Whole Body Fitness—Training Mind, Body, and Spirit*. New York: C. Potter, 1979.

Moore, Kenny. *Best Efforts: World Class Runners and Races*. New York: Doubleday, 1982.

——————————, "Watching Their Steps." *Sports Illustrated*, May 3, 1976.

Morgan, William P. "Test of Champions—The Iceberg Profile." *Psychology Today*, July, 1980, pp. 92–108.

——————————, "The Mind of the Marathoner." *Psychology Today*, April, 1978, pp. 39–49.

Moriarity, Bob. "Tom Tutko Interview." *Runner's World*, February, 1980, pp. 27–32.

185

Murphy, Michael. *Golf in the Kingdom.* New York: Dell, 1973.

_____, and White, Rhea A. *The Psychic Side of Sports.* Reading, Massachusetts. Addison Wesley, 1978.

Nideffer, Robert M. *The Inner Athlete: Mind Plus Muscle for Winning.* New York: Thomas Crowell, 1976.

Orlick, Terry. *In Pursuit of Excellence.* Champaign, Illinois: Human Kinetics, 1980.

Osler, Tom. *Serious Runner's Handbook.* Mountain View, California: Anderson World, 1978.

Pactor-Azor, Janet. "Optimizing Athletic Performance With Biofeedback Training." Princeton, New Jersey: Princeton Biofeedback Clinic, 1980. (mimeographed).

Parker, John L. "Dream Lovers." *Runner*, May, 1983, pp. 62–66.

Pelliccioni, Louis, Jr. and Scott, Michael D. *Don't Choke: How Athletes Can Become Winners.* Englewood Cliffs, New Jersey: Prentice-Hall, 1982.

Pirsig, Robert M. *Zen and the Art of Motorcycle Maintenance.* New York: William Morrow, 1974.

Porter, Donald. *Inner Running.* New York: Grosset and Dunlap, 1978.

Prokop, David. "The Inside Story of Hypnosis." *Runner's World*, September, 1981, pp. 39–43.

Restak, Richard M. *The Brain: The Last Frontier.* New York: Doubleday, 1979.

Rodgers, Bill. "Get Psyched." *Runner*, August 1980, p. 20.

Runner's World Magazine. *Guide To Sprinting.* Mountain View, California: World Publications, 1973.

Russell, Peter. *The Brain Book.* New York: Hawthorn Books, 1979.

Ryan, Frank. *Sports and Psychology.* Englewood Cliffs, New Jersey: Prentice-Hall, 1981.

Sacks, Michael H., and Sachs, Michael L., ed. *Psychology of Running.* Champaign, Illinois, Human Kinetics, 1981.

Sheldon, William. *Varieties of Human Physique.* New York: Harper, 1940.

Singer, Robert. *Myths and Truths in Sports Psychology.* New York: Harper and Row, 1975.

186

——————, "Thought Processes and Emotions in Sport." *Physician and Sports Medicine*, July, 1982, pp. 75–88.

Sheehan, George. *Running and Being*. New York: Simon and Schuster, 1978.

Spielberger, Charles D. *State-Trait Evaluation Questionnaire*. Palo Alto, California: Consulting Psychologists Press, 1968.

Spino, Mike. *Beyond Jogging—The Innerspaces of Running*. California: Celestial Arts, 1976.

——————, and Warren, Jeffrey Earl. *Mind/Body Running Program*. New York: Bantam Books, 1979.

Squires, Billy. *Improving Your Running*. Lexington, Massachusetts: Stephen Green, 1982.

Straub, William F., ed. *Sports Psychology—An Analysis of Athletic Behavior*. Ithaca, New York: Movement Publications, 1978.

Suinn, R., ed. *Psychology in Sports: Methods and Applications*. Minnesota: Burgess Press, 1980.

——————, "Body Thinking: Psychology for Olympic Champs." *Psychology Today*, July, 1976, pp. 38–43.

Suzuki, D. T. *Zen and Japanese Culture*. New York: Pantheon, 1959.

Swartz, Don and Wayne, Ron. "How to Mentally Prepare for Better Performances." *Runner's World*, 1979, pp. 90–95.

Temple, Cliff. "A Nice Bloke Breaks Through." *Runner*, October, 1982, pp. 40–48.

Thomas, Vaughn. *Science and Sport*. Boston: Little, Brown, 1970.

Tutko, Thomas A., and Tosi, Umberto. *Sports Psyching: Playing Your Best Game All of the Time*. Los Angeles: J. P. Tarcher, 1976.

——————, and Richards, Jack W. *Psychology of Coaching*. Boston: Allyn and Bacon, 1971.

——————, Lyon, Leland P., and Ogilvie, Bruce C., *Athletic Motivation Inventory*. San Jose, California: Institute of Athletic Motivation; 1969.

Weiner, Norbert. *The Human Use of Human Beings*. New York: Avon Books, 1950.

Wing, Pam. "Man as Marine Mammal". *Oceans*, March, 1981, pp. 26–27.

Winter, Bud. *Relax and Win*. San Diego: A. S. Barnes, 1981.

INDEX

Index

192